ZOE BELL PUBLISHING
3020 Prosperity Church Road
PMB 255b
Charlotte, NC 28269

Printed in the United States of America

Breathe: Days of Inspiration
Copyright © 2013 Myra Bellinger
Revised August 2023
All rights reserved.
ISBN: 9781072310761

All rights reserved, including the right to reproduce this book, or any portion thereof, in any form. No part of this book may be reproduced or transmitted in any form or by any means, electronic or mechanical, magnetic, chemical, optical, manual, or otherwise, including photocopying, recording, or by any information storage or retrieval system without written permission from the Publisher. All rights for publishing this book or portions thereof in other languages are contracted by the Publisher

DEDICATION

As strange as this may seem, I dedicate this book to ME and the Spirit of Courage, Faith and Obedience for finally completing the first of many to come.

I also dedicate this book to my husband, Gary Bellinger and children, David Josiah & Maya Zoe who inspires me daily to breathe and press forward.

Table of Contents

ACKNOWLEDGMENTS   8

FORWARD   10

INTRODUCTION   11

SEE   14
Day 1: Why Breathe?   15
Day 2: Your Assignment   19
Day 3: Breathe To Blast Off   21
Day 4: The Source   24
Day 5: Align Your life   27
Day 6: Renew Your Mind   30
Day 7: Know Who You Are   32
Day 8: Patterns & Systems   35

CONFESS   38
Day 9: Fight Like Hell   39
Day 10: Move out of the Way   44
Day 11: Live the High Life   47
Day 12: It's a Matter of Perspective   52
Day 13: Just Say, YES!   56
Day 14: Posture For A Miracle   59

BELIEVE   63
Day 15: Shine Your Light On Me   64
Day 16: The Force Is With You   67
Day 17: I Will Never Make You Ashamed   69
Day 18: The Contradiction of Your Faith   71
Day 19: Stop Worrying   75
Day 20: See "Love" Right   77
Day 21: Don't Live In Fear of Missing God   79
Day 22: You Can Know His Will   85
Day 23: Rescue 911   88

DO   92

Day 24: First Things First   93
Day 25: The Revelation of Kenny Rogers   97
Day 26: Risky Business   99
Day 27: A Lesson on Balance   103
Day 28: Stay the Course   107
Day 29: Let the Umpire Do His Job   110
Day 30: Smoke Screens & Real Fire   112
Day 31: Prayer Still Works! 115
Day 32: Better NOT Bitter   118
Day 33: I Cannot Afford to be Useless in this Season   122
Day 34: Lesson on Investment   125

BONUS FEATURE   131
From the Heart of Your Father   131

ACKNOWLEDGMENTS

It is a known fact that what God calls for, He provides for. Whatever is His will is most certainly His bill. I am eternally grateful to Him for placing in my life key players, the most awesomely creative and faith-filled team who have the ability to see, the tenacity to help birth and skills to get the job done. Your faith in me inspires me and breathes life into me daily. For every life that will be transformed and touched from this compilation of inspiring words, you share in the eternal reward. Thank you.

The Key Players –
I Give Special Recognition and My Eternal Thanks:

Proofreader
Janine Carter

My Breathe Dream Team

Nicole Albright
Cherelle Archie
Beatrice Heyward
Crystal McDonald
Shyann Roseboro
Sherveena Terry
Lakessha Windley

My Project Coordinator and Senior Editor, Rona M. Williams, who without your research, organization, and skills this dream may not have become a reality. You made this process an exciting journey. I pray God's hundred-fold return for the many sacrifices you have made and continue to make for the Kingdom of God. Know that your labor is not in vain.

FORWARD

BREATHE…you have been running on autopilot long enough and now it's time to live on purpose again. It's time to recapture all that the pressures life has depleted from you. This book comes straight from the heart and spirit of one of God's mightiest women on the scene today. God has allowed Myra to share her most awesome adventures with Him as she fulfills her divine assignment to help people realize that there is life beyond where they are now. Myra pens eloquently how she found a way to breathe again and rekindle "Zoë", the God-kind of life. She shows how you can revive your attitude, life and spirit through this impactful devotional. This book is for everyone that believes there is more to life than just merely existing day to day.

As her husband of 18 years, I have watched Myra go through a metamorphosis in her relationship with God. She is now the epitome of her book and what she has written did not come from study alone, but from personal experiences with God and others. Over and over again, I observed her executing and displaying the wisdom she shares in this book. She lives the words, "lead by example". In this book, she teaches you how to envision where you are going and inspires you to live your best life. I encourage you as you read this book, to not only read it, but also begin to BREATHE again!

Pastor Gary Bellinger
City of God Ministries International
Charlotte, North Carolina

INTRODUCTION

Deep within you are wells of resources; wealth, creative energy and ideas just waiting for you to tap into them. They are there to impact your life, help you maximize your purpose and change this world. "But, how do I find this reservoir?" you ask. "If it is within me, how do I access it? How do I begin the journey to find my purpose and live each day to its fullest?" I sometimes feel much like the little boy from the movie the Sixth Sense who whispered, "I see dead people… Walking around like regular people. They don't see each other. They only see what they want to see. They don't know they're dead." I see people who are alive with bodies, breathing air and often going through life aimlessly—with little focus, satisfaction, mere existence and untapped potential. There is more to life than merely existing. There is an automatic instinct to take into ourselves the necessary elements for a successful life, but many of us are like dead men walking, never taking time to inhale inspiration daily.

Most people who feel as though they are suffocating are actually experiencing anxiety and not a respiratory event. Suffocation is usually an expression of the anxiety and worry we experience as we face life's situations. Your chest tightens as your heart rate accelerates. That jittery feeling, shortness of breath, dizziness, profuse sweating and nausea all accompany the subtle fear that you just might be going crazy. It's the moment when you realize there is so much to do, fix, figure out, work around, solve and there is only one of you. It's the moment when you realize that although there is a laundry list of things to finish, you're not fulfilled by any of it. It's the moment you stop to ask yourself, "Why am I here?" Or it's the moment that you almost decide that running away and assuming a new identity may be your only hope for peace again. If you're lucky, someone is nearby who can coach you through the moment. But that is a temporary fix. In most cases, our inability to **breathe** (enjoy life) is due to our busy lives, lack of purpose, wrong priorities or lack of direction.

When we breathe, we inhale life. Not just life, we inhale the life of God. Our systems are recalibrated and refreshed in the moments we take each day to discover our God-given purpose and His direction for our lives. As a pastor, life coach and entrepreneur, I understand the value of knowing one's purpose: defining your mission in life. My personal mission statement (my God-given purpose) is to bring glory to God and to live my life to be a blessing to the lives of people. It is the reason why I wrote this book. Breathe is all about knowing your purpose and inhaling inspiration daily to help you fulfill that purpose. It's about exhaling anxiety and worry and inhaling peace and direction. As God's creation, you were given His creative ability and placed on the earth to have dominion, subdue, multiply and replenish. Life is supposed to be more than good. It's supposed to be supernaturally awesome! Tyler Perry's fictional character Madea is known for her uniquely amusing and to the point wisdom. While discussing life and the troubles we face, Madea said, "Life is supposed to happen." I agree, "Life is supposed to happen." but not to you, for you! Life is not just a screenplay of highs and lows, but everything that happens in our lives should move us along our journey to a place called destiny. Life is more than living. "Zoe" means the God kind of life. God wants all of His children to experience that kind of life. The God kind of life offers peace, success, fulfillment, joy and abundant living.

    Breathe: Days of Inspiration will refuel, refocus, refresh and recalibrate you as you embark on the journey to discovering your purpose and reaching your ultimate destiny. This book will give you the strength and wisdom you need to maximize your full potential. If your purpose is unknown, then maximizing your potential is impossible. **You must know who you are, why you were created and what you were created to do while on earth.** Don't worry. This doesn't happen all at once. Discovering your purpose and actually living it takes work. It takes making time to visualize you at your best and employing the necessary tools to make your dream a reality. To become successful in life there are a few foundational truths that you must embrace. It's a very simple to do list, but it requires fortified tenacity to accomplish it consistently.

You must CONFESS the right things in order to BELIEVE the right things, and DO the right things. But, it all hinges on your ability to focus and SEE it first.

Life is all about purpose and destiny colliding. Be inspired to maximize every moment of your life by fulfilling your purpose and destiny. Leave an awesome legacy in the Earth. Learn to Breathe again!

SEE

DAY 1: WHY BREATHE?

Why Breathe? God creatively worked for five days on his delight, His creation. He made light, the heavens, the seas, dry land, and herb yielding seed. He made fruit trees, grass, the sun, the moon and the stars. With one command, He filled the seas with all sea creatures and birds to fly in and occupy the air. He blessed all of His creation and He instructed every fruit-bearing tree, sea creature, foul, cattle and every living thing to reproduce after its own kind. After five days of creating and speaking, commanding and blessing, God prepared himself for the climatic height of His creative work. On the sixth day, He prepared himself to make His most extraordinary creation: Man.

Then God said, "Let Us make man in Our image, according to Our likeness; let them have dominion over the fish of the sea, over the birds of the air, and over the cattle, over all the earth and over every creeping thing that creeps on the earth. So God created man in His own image; in the image of God He created him; male and female He created them. (Genesis 1:26-27 NKJV)
And the LORD God formed man of the dust of the ground, and breathed into his nostrils the breath of life; and man became a living being. (Genesis 2:7 NKJV)

Picture this: There was just a lifeless, dead, dusty, gray looking corpse after God formed man from the dust of the ground. It was not until God *breathed* into his nostrils that this lifeless corpse came into being; he came to life. He became a living soul!

Think deeper now. This man already had God's image, His form and His likeness, but when God breathed into Him, this man then received the eternal and creative life of God inside of him! He is now alive with the LIFE, NATURE and ABILITY of God! Man is now fully calibrated to live in the earth with the divine nature of God! He is a living soul!

We are living today with the life, nature and ability of God inside of us. Do this exercise with me. Inhale. Come on...take in a deep, slow breath right now. You have the creative force...the creative ability of God inside of you right now. Slowly exhale. If you just completed those breaths properly, fresh oxygen went to each of your cells, both naturally and spiritually. Man is a multicellular being with an estimated 37.2 trillion cells. Each cell is an amazing world unto itself: it can take in nutrients, convert these nutrients into energy, carry out specialized functions, and reproduce as necessary. Even more amazing is that each cell stores its own set of instructions for carrying out each of these activities.

All too often because of life and its challenges, we do not breathe as often as we should and we seldom breathe properly. Proper oxygenation to our cells (naturally and spiritually) is necessary for our amazing bodies to perform at maximum capacity. That's what BREATHE is all about. It is about slowing down, with the right posture and tapping into the lifeline and life source inside of you so that you can produce maximum results in life.

Most of us know the story of the creation, if not, read Genesis chapters 1-3. After God blew the breath of life into Adam, God gave Adam a job.

> The LORD God took the man and put him in the Garden of Eden to work it and take care of it. And the LORD God commanded the man, "You are free to eat from any tree in the garden; but you must not eat from the tree of the knowledge of good and evil, for when you eat from it you will certainly die." The LORD God said, "It is not good for the man to be alone. I will make a helper suitable for him." Now the LORD God had formed out of the ground all the wild animals and all the birds in the sky. He brought them to the man to see what he would name them; and whatever the man called each living creature, that was its name. So the man gave names to all the livestock, the birds in the sky and all the wild animals. But for Adam no suitable helper was

found. **So the LORD God caused the man to fall into a deep sleep; and while he was sleeping, he took one of the man's ribs and closed up the place with flesh.** Then the LORD God made a woman from the rib he had taken out of the man, and he brought her to the man. (Genesis 2:15-22 NIV)

(Just a sidebar for the ladies---if your Adam is sleeping, please leave Him alone! There is a purpose for his slumber. You just make sure you are maximizing your time alone with God while he is asleep)!

Man & woman together had total dominion. They knew everything. They named everything. They were over everything on the earth, but the tempter came in the form of a DISTRACTION. Immediately, all of the dominion, life, nature, creativity and ability of God was lost in an instant. It was lost as the result of a conversation with a snake—a snake that they named and had dominion over. Really? I believe they were smart enough to avoid losing their God nature to a lowly creeping creature over which they had dominion. I do not believe it was a literal snake. You do not have to agree with my theology, but I believe it was something greater than any earthly being that they had ever seen before. It was something that they did not recognize and therefore did not know they had dominion over. They did not name this being. This being was different from them and something about Him was attractive or at least stirred their curiosity. I believe it was Lucifer himself. He was beautiful and unusual—something outside of the sphere of their understanding and influence. Lucifer was different and He got their attention. (Read Ezekiel 28 & Isaiah 14)

What they experienced that day is not different from what you and I experience on a daily basis when we are distracted. **Siding with even one distraction against the will of God can cause you to lose it all.** Adam and Eve fell and lost all, but Jesus came to restore ALL! BREATHE is about embracing the creative force of God and your life in Him. Breathe is about living and operating in your dominion and position as both a king and a priest. It is about taking dominion and rightly receiving, releasing, and activating what is in you.

Make breathing a part of your daily life. Take a moment each day to just 'Breathe'. Have pen and paper handy. Find a quiet, still place. Breathe in and out, again & again; and clear your mind. Then watch what happens to your life. When you do this daily, you will find how easily direction, peace, rest, creativity, witty inventions, creative ideas, new life, hope and help flow through you, for you. Remember, one God-idea can take you from rags to riches; from turmoil to peace; and from defeat to victory. Just breathe then breathe again.

Scripture Meditations: Genesis 1:2, Job 32:6

DAY 2: YOUR ASSIGNMENT

I want to share with you one of the greatest challenges ever! I want to give you an assignment. I know you are probably busy with a lot of stuff to do. Maybe you have got so much going on you feel as if you do not have enough time to get anything else done. However, I promise that this assignment will be the one constant commitment you will want to make to yourself! Make this a major part of your daily life--not something that you occasionally do. When you fully grasp the power of this assignment, you will see how necessary it is and how it is—as important as breathing!

If there is no breath in us then there is no life, right? This will fuel the vehicle designed to get you to where you want to go—the expected end the Father has designed for you. You will see that this assignment will be a source of life to you and your visions and dreams. This assignment is something you must do for the rest of your life. All successful people do it! Are you ready? I want you to stop everything, find a comfortable spot, breathe and then begin to envision! "Envision?" Yes indeed, ENVISION. That is your challenge and assignment.

I love this word, envision. It makes me realize that there is something that is IN ME (en-vision); an inward vision that I need for my success. It is something that I have total control over regardless of my external situations. The power to achieve and fulfill my destiny is in me. I could give you many words to define success. Several ingredients make up the final product of success. The simplest definition for success is achieving and fulfilling one's purpose. I know people who are always looking to something or someone else for direction for success, but only the creator of a thing really knows its intended purpose. When we take the time to silence our world, quiet ourselves, and focus in on our core, then we are truly able to see, hear and know the proper course for our individual success.

To envision means to picture mentally, especially some future event or events: to envision a bright future. Wow! This one act is the foundation for success. To envision where you are going and how you are going to get there is a pivotal consideration and factor in the outcome of your success. It determines whether you really will get there. You see, the way the principle works is this: **"You've got to see it (inside), before you see it, or you never will see it!"**

Scripture Meditations: Proverbs 18:21, Romans 10:8, Joshua 1:8, Isaiah 43:19, Isaiah 55:10

DAY 3: BREATHE TO BLAST OFF

"But the people that do know their God will be strong and do exploits." Daniel 11:32

On July 20, 1969 at 4:18 p.m. EST, Neil Armstrong said, "The Eagle Has Landed." In addition, at 10:56 p.m., Armstrong, descending from Eagle's ladder and touching one foot to the Moon's surface, announced, "That's one small step for a man, one giant leap for mankind." This was man's first dramatic venture on the lunar surface. Can you imagine what was going through the minds of the three astronauts, Aldrin, Armstrong and Collins on board Apollo 11 as they prepared for this launch? Can you imagine the anticipation in the air of all who were monitoring and viewing this historic event? The voyage began on July 16th at approximately 9:30 a.m. in the morning. It took four and a half days before this dream became a reality. This does not include all the years of research, investigation, test launches and the teams of people over the years that helped to make this a reality. The launch began with a countdown to a blast-off, and 50 years later, at the point of this writing, to view this blast off experience through historic video footage or to read about it still creates excitement. This launch created a history-making, life changing moment that left an eternal legacy.

That is what God always has in mind for His most extraordinary creation: man. After five days of creating and speaking, commanding and blessing, God prepared himself for the climatic height of His creative work. On the sixth day, when God made man, He BREATHED into him every creative function and ability that man would ever need to be fruitful, to multiply, to subdue and to have dominion in the earth. He gave man an amazing body and an amazing creative mind! He expects man to follow His commands and always remain on the launching pad of life ready for new depths, higher heights and life-long legacies.

In order to get the most inspiration from your time with BREATHE, you must know that the Creator wants you to always be in position and ready to blast off to the next place destined for you. His desire is that you would become so in sync with the Powers of the Universe that you do exploits. His desire is that you are always moving from faith to faith and from glory to glory. As you spend time breathing, remember these three rules:

1. Be OPEN – Be open to new ideas, new thoughts, mindsets and new ways of doing things. The Power of the Universe is going to challenge you to open up to new experiences, new people, new places and new things.

2. Be FREE – Quiet your world and free your mind of all outside distractions, judgments, responsibilities, anxieties and worries. These are all forbidden thoughts, especially during your breathing times.

3. Be FRIENDLY – The Holy Spirit is the God in the Earth today. It is His wisdom that you will inhale. Be Friendly to Him. Recognize that He is a person who is always present with you. Enjoy fellowship with Him. Always be aware of His indwelling presence. Obey Him quickly and write down things that He speaks to you or brings to your mind, with awareness that the moments He shares with us is special. Understand that He is not obligated to speak the same things again and again. Be intentional, be deliberate, and do everything He shows you, the way He shows you.

Blastoff, according to the dictionary, is the launching of a rocket under its own power and the time at which this occurs. Imagine that you are the rocket and in you is the power to blast off. As you diligently do all the Holy Spirit tells you, there is a perfect timing for all things. One of the things I have learned about God is that He is not governed by time, but He is a God of timing. That means that He moves at a time and pace to produce the most effective results. We are in partnership with Him. We must be in position, doing our part, so that He can actively do His part. Unfortunately, God is blamed for many things that are not His fault.

Many Christians are "waiting" on God to act, but God is waiting on them to "work" and to "know Him" so that they can be strong and do exploits!

What you do every day matters. When you spend time daily breathing in God's presence, you will find that you will be refueled, refocused, recalibrated, and refreshed. Fresh ideas and witty inventions will come to you. Spending time in His presence is like taking a daily mini vacation out of this world to hear what He is saying to you for every season and situation of your life. When you consistently spend time with Him, you will never again miss a window of opportunity. You will even find quick solutions to the things that seem to catch you off guard. You may feel that you do not have enough time to breathe daily, but you must make time because YOU matter! Only the creator of a thing really knows its intended purpose. By spending time breathing in God's presence, you come to know your purpose in life and that only you can fulfill that purpose. You can only fulfill that purpose correctly with His clear instructions.

Scripture Meditations: Daniel 11:23, Ephesians 1

DAY 4: THE SOURCE

Remember the source of your vision (envisioning) comes from the Creator. When you practice this discipline, your life will really begin to change. Proverbs 23: 7a (NKJV) says as a man "thinks in his heart [spirit], so is he." Your life is all about perspective. How do you see your life? Is the glass half-empty or half-full? Usually the person whose life is full of negativity sees the glass half-empty. Have you ever heard the weather report say that there is a fifty percent chance of rain today and you were instantly convinced that it was definitely going to rain? Did you ever stop to consider that there was also a fifty percent chance that it would not rain? We must not allow negative thinking to control and shape our perspectives. Our perspective and speech really matters and helps to determine our outcome. The only way we can live free from negativity and with proper perspective is to tap into the Source of our existence and vision.

We must be kingdom-minded citizens while living on earth. Matthew 6:10 (KJV) says, "thy kingdom come, thy will be done on earth as it is in heaven." Here is a practical example. Do you remember when President Barack Obama took office? According to all reports, America was facing the worst economic recession since the Great Depression. In my time of breathing, I understood that although I am IN this world, I am not OF this world; therefore, the rules of this world's system do not apply to me. My kingdom mindset kicked in and said, 'Since there is no recession in the Kingdom of Heaven, I do not have to agree with the fact that the recession may affect me.' I did not accept recession as my truth. Just because America was facing a dark time did not mean that my family and I were going to experience a dark time. Gary and I believed all our needs would be supplied; and they were. God supplied every need during that time, and many of our wants too! Our family lived better than ever! That would not have been possible if we did not take the time to envision and tap into God's ideas, plans and resources for us. We refused to confess and agree with recession, but instead spent a lot of time saying, "There is no recession in the Kingdom!" When days seem bleak and your vision is obscure, close your natural eyes and ears, and open your spiritual eyes and ears long enough to see and hear what the Spirit of the Lord is saying to you concerning your life.

Here are some practical things I encourage you to do when you are envisioning:

- **Journal. Make sure you have purchased the accompanying Breathe Journal.** It is designed to go along with this daily devotional. In the journal, I share with you the exact steps to take to "Breathe Properly." It is a working journal that will help you to discover and sharpen your purpose and potential in the earth. The journal works through each day of Breathe and provides space for you to write down thoughts, ideas, questions, suggestions, scriptures, songs, etc. that may come to mind during this time. Always date your breathing/envisioning sessions. Remember, God is not obligated to speak again so you must value this time with Him.

- **Clear your mind.** Take the problem out of the equation when listening for solutions or directions. Here is how I do this. I ask myself, "If ____ (the problem) did not exist, what would I do?" Your questions may sound like this: 'What would I do if I loved my job? What would I do if I had all the money I needed to accomplish every dream I have? What would I do if I did not have to work on this job every day?' Write down your answers.

- **Write the Vision.** Once you have a clear vision of where to go and what to do, find a visual image of it. This could be a picture, a confession, a business plan or anything that will inspire you to reach your goals. Write your dream on paper and explain as much of it as you can now. God is progressive. His vision for you is bigger than you think. As you continue to envision and work toward the vision, God will reveal more. Your vision will expand as you go. Review your visuals as often as possible because seeing it helps you 'see' it.

- **Speak it.** Make sure every confession; every word that you speak aligns with the reality of that vision. I do not care how difficult things become. Let your words be consistent with what you know in your heart.

- **Dare to do it!** Make immediate strides towards reaching your new goals. Get busy doing the work. Faith without works is dead. Work means:

    o Doing your research
    o Finding those who are doing it and learn what you can from them
    o Making divine connections
    o Changing habits that hinder you from accomplishing your goals

- **Get ready for a good fight!** Opposition is sure to come. Stand and fight! Do not wimp out! Anything worth having is worth fighting for.

- **Prevent Self-sabotage.** Make sure you are not your own worst enemy.

- **Don't Settle.** Settle for nothing less than the promise!

Scripture Meditations: Ephesians 6:10, I Timothy 6:12, Habakkuk 2:2

DAY 5: ALIGN YOUR LIFE

Besides spending time breathing, what else do I need to do to maximize my purpose and capacity in life? I am glad you asked. You must align your life to **breathe properly**. The following list is what I have learned while breathing in His presence. I am certain these things will help transform your life as well.

- STOP MAKING EXCUSES! Stop making excuses about why you cannot do something or why you do not have enough time or money to get it done. That is unacceptable. Ask the Holy Spirit to give you the resolve to get it done.

- BEWARE OF DISTRACTIONS! Stop being so busy and putting everyone and everything else before you. That is what is sapping you of your strength, health, ability to focus and God's creative energy.

- GET RID OF CLUTTER! Clutter can be anything from a lot of junk around you to a schedule or calendar that is too busy. Maybe you or the people that depend on you are involved in too many activities. Declutter your life, your environment and leave room in your schedule for new things and the gift of spontaneity.

- SHUT DOWN ALL SOURCES OF NEGATIVITY! Recognize that not everyone can go where you are going. If there is anything or anyone who breeds negativity, shut them down by refusing to allow their thoughts to penetrate your belief system. Do not use your energy trying to change them or convince them of positive things. Do whatever you must to refute their negative spirit.

- BUILD YOUR RELATIONSHIP WITH GOD! Do not waste all of your time in His presence asking for things. Although exhaling is necessary, remember, "Breathe" is also about inhaling: spending more time listening. When He does not seem to be communicating or speaking, love Him enough just to rest and relax in His presence. That is real relationship.

- TAKE TIME TO ENVISION! **Envisioning is tapping into the God-sense in you.** It is yielding to the creative force of God in you. God gave us a pattern in the book of beginnings to help us produce his commands to be fruitful, to multiply, to subdue and to have dominion. God spent six days working (creating, speaking, commanding & blessing) and then was able to rest on the seventh day. These are our instructions. Adhering to these principles helps us follow God's plan and will for our lives. In the next few days of inspiration, I will share more about the envisioning process. These concepts are shaping my life and impacting my destiny.

The last step to aligning your life to breathe properly is….

- LIVE EVERY DAY IN EXPECTATION! Expectation is the breeding ground for miracles. Expectation is really Bible hope. It is not wishing things might happen. It is expecting them to happen every day! Your faith is the switch that turns God on. Your faith will make all the powers of the universe respond to you. Your faith is like dynamite. It will create an explosion and manifest what you desire. The believer seldom suffers from a lack of faith. Our problem quickly becomes our lack of hope. For many, after they have expected for so long, expectation dwindles and pretty soon, there is little to no hope. The belief system of "well, we know God can, but we feel like He just might not do it for me," slowly but powerfully creeps and settles in. That belief system is perpetuated by a mindset that says it is okay to think this way, because after all, He is God and He can do what He chooses. This is a trick of the enemy. The bible says "hope deferred makes the heart sick, but when the desire comes, it is a tree of life." Proverbs 13:12 (NKJV) Faith is your stick of dynamite, but hope (expectation) is the fuse to your stick of dynamite. One without the other is no good. My advice is to keep the power of expectation on the rise. Do not let the enemy steal from you by robbing you of your hope. Keep hope alive.

Scripture Meditations: Romans 5:3-5, Proverbs 13:12, I Corinthians 15:58

DAY 6: RENEW YOUR MIND

Hopefully, you have begun the envisioning process. This process really begins with renewing the mind. Renewing the mind means that you believe what God says in His Word concerning you. It does not matter what people, situations and circumstances say. Believing God takes work. It requires a lot of meditation to change your thoughts and mindsets.

This powerful tool of envisioning is not daydreaming by far! Webster's Dictionary defines a daydream as "a pleasant visionary usually *wishful creation of the imagination*." "Daydreaming is a short-term detachment from one's immediate surroundings, during which a person's contact with reality is blurred and partially substituted by a visionary fantasy, especially one of happy, pleasant thoughts, hopes or ambitions, imagined as coming to pass, and experienced while awake." (Wikipedia) **Envisioning is much deeper than the concept of daydreaming.** Daydreaming only produces a temporary change in feeling and outlook, and requires a temporary detachment of reality. Envisioning is so much more than a feeling and a detachment from what is real. When you envision, your vision is not blurred, but clear. Envisioning is all about tapping into the reality of what the God of the Universe sees in you and desires for you.

Envisioning is powerful. That is why the enemy has a counterfeit for it. He does all he can to keep you from envisioning. The counterfeit is daydreaming. The distractions from your spiritual reality are his weapons of defeat. Think about it. You are constantly distracted with things that keep you busy—often too busy to do the things that really matter, and envisioning really matters. We must find the time to quiet ourselves, tap into the depths of our spirit to get clear instructions and directions straight from heaven.

You may not know it, but the things of this world are temporary. Our world is a Matrix of sorts. If you have never seen the movie, I suggest you do. I just love that movie because it illustrates what is really going on between our experienced natural reality and our spiritual reality. Everything in the world that we see has come from a permanent and more real world that we cannot see. God spoke this world into existence by the power of His thoughts and words. That same creative power is in you! God gave it to you! You have the power to create your world. When you believe and 'see' what you speak, before you actually see the manifestation of what you have spoken, then you are operating in your God-given supernatural ability to envision.

Daydreaming in itself is not bad. It is just not productive. After the daydream is over, there is not a decisive call to action. There is no direction. There is no change. But, when you envision, change takes place. When you envision, you not only see the end result, you see steps and actions you must take to get there. Envisioning inspires you to act. It creates a desire in you to make your dream a reality. As you envision your future, trust that God will give you the strategies and action steps needed to make that future a reality.

Scripture Meditations: Romans 12:1-2, Job 32:8, 2 Corinthians 4:16-18, Joshua 1:8

DAY 7: KNOW WHO YOU ARE

It does not matter where you come from. It does not matter how much money you have in the bank. It does not matter what anyone says or thinks about you. The power to be successful lies within you and begins with the process of envisioning! The real you is an eternal spirit being that gets its life source from its Creator. As a believer, the Creator lives on the inside of you. And, you, the real you, gets its life source and information from the Creator who knows EVERYTHING. There is nothing you need to know, that you cannot know. We must renew our minds and know:

- Who we are
- Whose we are
- What we have
- What we can do

Who are you? If you are a child of God, you are the righteousness of God in Him. That means you do not fear, are not inferior and know no defeat! You are a joint heir with Jesus Christ. You share everything that belongs to Him. He supplies all of your needs. You are not just a human being—you are a human-divine being. You are a god in the earth today. You execute God's will and reign by use of His authority and power. He has given you the power to reign and rule in this life!

Whose are you? Wealth and privilege is often generational. Most often, those distinctions are seldom associated with someone because of their own accomplishments but rather, because of birthright. Wealth is most often a birthright, a state of living one enjoys because of their birth. That family relationship introduces you to a life of privilege & wealth. When we understand whose we are, the family we are born into when receiving salvation, we understand how privileged and wealthy we truly are. You belong to the Creator and Owner of the Universe who has all authority and all power! He loves you. He cares for you. He created you with destiny and purpose. Begin to reflect on all that God is and all that you are. You belong to a great & mighty God. You are a peculiar people, a royal priesthood. You sit in heavenly places with God. You are not ordinary or common. You are special because you belong to the King of Kings & Lord of Lords. He is your God and you are His people. You are the apple of God's eye. Affirm your identity by understanding your relationship with Him. That relationship gives you great value. Enough said. Meditate on that.

What do I have and what can I do? Everything and anything. The best choices are what God desires you to have. I know that is a difficult thing to grasp. You have everything and can do anything. There are universal principles and laws that work for or against you. You do not have to believe in the law of gravity for it to work. It just works. Because of the principles of the universe, you can obtain things that God does not particularly want you to have. A perfect example in the Bible is Israel and their desire for a king. A king was not God's desire for them, but they kept asking, envisioning, confessing for a King and they eventually got a King. But, a human natural king was not God's best for them.

Desire the things God wants for you and do things God has created you to do. You will find happiness, fulfillment & joy when you embrace the will of God for your life. There is no greater place of safety & peace than His will. God has empowered you with the Holy Spirit who gives you the wisdom of God. That wisdom brings us into immeasurable success. He warns us, gives us direction & comfort. We are then able to make our own way prosperous as opportunities arise and experience good success. Joshua 1:8 (KJV)

These are foundational principles for success. I want you to renew your mind today and begin the process of envisioning your life. Conceptualize what this envisioning process entails and then begin to do it now! Change what you see in the natural by tapping into what is on the inside of you. Tap into the Creator's thoughts and visions for you and your life. Envision a better future. Envision your life differently. Envision your dreams fulfilled. Envision what life would be like if money were inexhaustible. Envision your future generations as the success story God has purposed! When you do this, you will begin to see the powers of the universe respond to what you see and your success will manifest in reality. This is not a New Age doctrine; it is God's faith principles at work in the life of every believer who will dare to embrace these principles. Meet me tomorrow. I cannot wait to continue this time with you.

Scripture Meditations: Romans 12:1, Proverbs 18:21, II Peter 1:3, II Corinthians 2:1

DAY 8: PATTERNS & SYSTEMS

The Cambridge Dictionary defines a pattern this way:

"a **particular** way in which something is done or **organized**, or in which something **happens**."

    Sometimes, I get what I call these "wonderful downloads" from a power much greater than I. It is as if the Heavens open to me and a wisdom far greater than my natural ability comes to me. It's amazing and supernatural. I can recall the day I received the inspiration that I am about to share with you. Once I meditated on it and continued to share this wisdom with others, it became quite obvious that this reality is a life-changing certainty. Here's the wisdom.

    There are recognizable, identifiable PATTERNS in which each of us have operated in life. These patterns can be observed by anybody. These patterns are observed especially by the enemy of your soul and all those forces of evil designed to hinder your progress. The enemies of your soul can be people who are jealous of you, your proverbial "haters" or the devil himself. They watch you. They study you. They are very familiar with you. Then, at the most inopportune moment, they use your own patterns against you to hinder your progress and productivity. It is as if they have a remote to your life and they are very skilled and quite timely in pushing all the right buttons at the wrong time to produce their desired and epic ending: No progress & No forward motion for you! They really don't have a remote, but we have unconsciously given them power.

    Think about it. Almost every time you get ready to move forward… to launch out into the deep…..to do something great, the same things…the same negative energy comes to sap you of energy and to hinder your productivity. These challenges come to distract you from the leap! Usually it's someone or something close to you that does something to hinder or injure you somehow. Your relationships with your spouse, children, friends or family members become challenged. It could be that you experience sudden "emergencies," fear, lack, defeat, jealousy, anger, frustration, discouragement, rejection, abandonment, sickness and the like.

It is a true fact that the forces of evil can hinder us! There is a scripture found in the Holy Bible that says, *"….we wanted to come to you—…again and again—but Satan hindered us."* 1 Thessalonians 2:18 English Standard Version (ESV)
While that may be true, here is what I know. Negative forces can try to block us but the reality is, they can't stop us! Only we can stop the process of our forward motion. This happens when we surrender to the forces working against us. We must learn to fight, stand and press!

I often decree, "I am in this world but I am not of this world and the rules of this world will not dictate anything to me!" I am not natural. I am supernatural; therefore **I have the power to erect new systems to eradicate old patterns!** That's a great declaration for you to make right now! Release the energy. Say it aloud: **I have the power to erect new systems to eradicate old patterns!**

The Cambridge Dictionary defines a system this way:

a set of connected items or devices that operate together:

a way of doing things; a method:

We have to create systems that change our old patterns! We must live in light of the fact that we should always be evolving, growing, and changing. This reality requires a shift in our perspectives. What worked before, may not work now. I have learned, in order to expand my capacity, I must challenge myself to change. Change requires an exchange of old patterns and the building of new systems. I have the ability to erect NEW SYSTEMS to eradicate old patterns! This is often more difficult than it sounds, but very possible. When you have to have a CHANGE OF MINDSET it will produce a CHANGE OF MOUTH SET.

As you prepare to produce the new and great things that are coming to you during your times of BREATHING, expect to see patterns. Make a pact with yourself. When you see or feel the old stuff coming up that has always defeated you every other time you were on the road to progress, get happy and SHOUT and FIGHT. This is a new system that you are erecting. See this as a sign from the universe that you are on the right track!!! Get happy! Persevere and keep it moving! Bump the dumb stuff! You've got this.

Scripture Meditation: 2 Corinthians 4:18, I Timothy 6:12, Philippians 3:14-15

CONFESS

DAY 9: FIGHT LIKE HELL

Have you ever felt beckoned by something greater than you? Can't you feel it? Something is tugging on you...calling you to a different place. It's a place you have never been before yet, with anticipation, you want to go. You have not seen this place but you feel it. This place you sense is vast. It is unknown but you know it is great. It is a higher place. It is your destiny calling you up and out of the box. What is the box? The box is anything that restricts you. The box limits your potential and confines you to familiar sources of knowledge and circles of influence. The box, until this point, was not bad. It was actually good for you because the box brought you to the place where you are now. Previously, the box served as a mode of transportation that brought you to your current place in life. But now, there is a Force that is breaking you out of the box and taking you to your new place of destiny.

There is a price to pay to get out of the box. Some people never will reach their destiny because they simply lack what it takes. They are unwilling to pay the price. The hardest thing about breaking out of the box is the unfortunate loss of people and things that are close to us so we can pursue the "tug" or "destiny" that we must fulfill. You don't want to lose anything or anybody, but sometimes in order to gain you must first lose. There is something within us a basic need or desire for those close to us to understand us, compliment and to celebrate us. At times, we find that they are unable to understand the choices we make in pursuit of our destiny. Often we try to explain ourselves and our need for companionship along the journey fulfilled by them, but to no avail. We spend countless amounts of energy trying to be accepted. Trying to get everyone on our bandwagon often becomes an energy sapping, non-productive feat, so we decide to go it alone. Ours is a heartfelt journey. There is a cry that comes from deep within us that says, "Help! I really want to be understood by you. I am on my way to my place of destiny and I don't want to go without you. My hour is at hand. I'm closer than I've ever been. I've paid a dear price for this place in time so I'm not willing to miss my window of opportunity, my season or my portal to this open heaven. I really need you here, but if you're unwilling to help, support and celebrate my journey, I must let you go. This place is not about me, it's about us. Don't let me go alone!"

Doesn't this sound like Jesus' experience in the Garden of Gethsemane? (Matthew 26:36-45) He took the disciples who were closest to him, perhaps hoping that they would be able to help Him in the critical moment where decision meets destiny. He hoped they would support Him as He broke out of the box of religious constraint into a new journey that would guarantee spiritual freedom for all. But they couldn't. They were unable to understand the gravity of the moment and therefore, when they should have been praying and interceding for Him they were asleep. When you feel like this, know that you are in your garden experience. Usually when you reach this place, you must go the rest of the way alone with only the wind of the grace of God to propel you and the angels of the Lord to strengthen you.

What you'd most like to say to those closest to you in these times is, "I am like a mother with child who is ready to deliver at any moment and I am experiencing all the sensitivities that go along with labor. You don't understand the anticipation, restlessness, sleeplessness, discomfort, anxiety and frustration of wanting to get this baby out of me. I am extremely sensitive. I am keenly aware that I am on the brink of something great and awesome." Even if you could express all of that, usually they are unable to relate to this place and without intention, become a source of pain and disappointment.

We must be watchful because those whom we love the most can become the source of distraction. One distraction caused Adam and Eve to lose their focus and position. Distractions of any sort cannot be tolerated when we are in hot pursuit of our destiny. There is a psyche, a disposition, a mindset that is required to break out of the box. You must be single-minded, knowing that you are branded by your Creator! You must seize the moment and maximize your full potential in life. I ministered during the pastoral celebration of a dear friend, Co-Pastor Darlene Mickens, whose event theme was "Purposed, Poised and Positioned to Move Forward". You must be purposed, poised and positioned to move forward! Those words impacted me so much that I have included and defined them for you to help you gain the strength and disposition needed to move to your next dimension.

Purposed: the object toward which one strives or for which something exists; an aim or a goal

Poised: having a self-assured manner; having a graceful and elegant bearing

Positioned: put or arrange (someone or something) in a particular place or way

Move forward: to advance with something; to make progress with something

Branded: to mark with or as if with a hot iron; to mark to show ownership; to impress firmly; fix ineradicably

Single-minded: Having one overriding purpose or goal; steadfast; *resolute (*firm in purpose or belief; characterized by firmness and determination*)

      When you comprehend and embrace the terms above, you understand that you must get out of the box. You must be poised knowing that you have been positioned to move forward. You are branded by a Force far greater than you therefore, you must be single-minded to reach your destiny. Once the proper psyche and disposition is gained, you must ask the question, "How do I break out of the box?" The simple answer is that you've got to fight like hell against Hell and all of its forces!

      Fight against the spirit of familiarity, complacency, distraction and fear. None of these things can be tolerated, not from your peers, family or even yourself. Fight against yourself; your soul (which encompasses your mind, will and emotions). Recognize that you cannot settle for your current position in life. This "tug" or "call" to destiny is spiritual. It is beyond your feelings. It is beyond what you can see; therefore, you must dig deeper into your core to receive this new direction for life.

Fight in a resolute fashion, standing strong against everything and anything that will try to deter you from your destiny. Fight with every fiber of your being; with strength and tenacity. Cooperate 100 percent with the Holy Spirit (that voice on the inside of you) and with the angels assigned to you. God knows the road ahead, so allow Him to lead and guide you. Realize that controlling your situation and relinquishing control at the same time just doesn't work. They are opposing actions. Let God drive your life and trust that He knows what is best for you. You must fight to enter into His rest. When we are able to rest and stop striving we experience peace. In the original Hebrew the phrase "cease striving" indicates giving up by letting our hands down. This means that we cannot hold the steering wheel and let God drive at the same time. When we release the wheel, we experience the peace that comes from trust.

Fight with clear vision. Do not tolerate negative thoughts. Write the vision and make it plain. Meditate on it and keep the vision before you as inspiration for your journey. Post messages and reminders where you can see them and say them aloud. Continue to write the vision as more is revealed to you. Exchange your vision for your life with God's vision for your life. Agree with what God says about you. Fight the good fight of faith with your actions and not just your words. Do something different to defy the status quo each day. As you fight with your words and actions, be careful not to reverse the effectiveness of your pursuit by saying negative things about your life, family or finances. Remember that you are well equipped, motivated, prepared and strengthened for the fight to break out of your box and reach your place of destiny. Confess truth based truth upon the Word of the Lord to you and for you!

Lose everything that is a distraction from your purpose and focus on all the blessings the promise will bring. That is exactly what Jesus did. Accept your "cup", stay focused and go ahead, leap out of the box! If Jesus didn't take a leap of faith into his purpose, where would we all be today? Jesus realized that "it is necessary that I go so that the greater can come to pass." Come on, leap! Fight like hell and get out of that box! You can do it and you will be glad you did. Shalom!

Scripture Meditations: Psalm 19:14, 66, 46:10, 141:3, Proverbs 18:21, Mark 11:24

DAY 10: MOVE OUT OF THE WAY

Have you ever auditioned for the role of "Holy Ghost, Jr."? It's a one-act play that usually ends in disaster. You know what that's like, right? It's that moment when you realize that you have done all you know to do and find out that what should have worked ended in complete failure. Or that it is not happening in the timing "Holy Ghost, Jr." anticipated. So what do you do? You kick into super hero mode and use your non-super powers to take matters to the next level. You try to make things happen by your own might and strength because you are certain God needs your help! Well, the truth of the matter is He does not need your help! God is God alone and prefers that you just move out of His way and allow Him to be the only God in your life.

Often we are nervous and anxious about the future. Sometimes in life, things change mid-stream and our plans are not fulfilled. We must not forget that He is God and God alone! The background noise and uncertainties in life often distracts us from what is most important. God will not share His throne with another. He rules well from His throne. Do you really think God does not know about unexpected curves in the road or unplanned pit stops along your journey? Absolutely not! Nothing catches Him by surprise! God anticipates and plans for every situation and circumstance in your life. There is no situation too big for Him to handle. There is absolutely NOTHING that he does not know!

One of my favorite passages in the scripture is Psalm 139:16, especially when I am feeling overwhelmed or uncertain about uncharted territory. "You saw me before I was born. Every day of my life was recorded in your book. Every moment was laid out before a single day had passed." (New Living Translation) The Message Bible says it this way, "Like an open book, you watched me grow from conception to birth, all the stages of my life were spread out before you, The days of my life all prepared before I'd even lived one day." That is amazing. It is my proof that I'm just going through the motions! I really am walking backwards from my future into my present. If it's previously recorded, that means it's already completed! He has prepared every stage and every moment of my life. Nothing I experience is a surprise to God. No matter what stands before me, no matter what I am facing, no matter the uncertainty, He knows and has a plan in mind for me.

I've often wondered how God speaks in a past tense and not lie? I know it is impossible for Him to lie. But, He just doesn't always seem to be telling the whole truth based upon what I can see from my vantage point. Here's an example of what I mean. God said to Abraham, "I have made thee the father of many nations," even before he had a child. "Have made" is the present perfect tense, meaning an action happened at an unspecified time before now. The exact time is not important. God changed both Sarai and Abram's name to Sarah and Abraham, aligning the universe with what He already established in the heavens. (Sarah means mother of a multitude or Princess and Abraham means father of many nations.) At the time, they still didn't have a child. God spoke about their situation as if it were a reality because He changed it in the past. It was already done!

That's the revelation that we must embrace about our God daily; rejoicing and living fully assured of His ability to move for us when we move out of His way. I have decided to embrace the reality that nothing touches my life that God is not aware of and for which He does not already have a way of escape. It is impossible for Him to fail. We must recognize that what God says about our future, our lives, our finances, our businesses, our children is truth regardless of what we see! God speaks in the perfect present tense because when He speaks, He releases sufficient faith to cause it to come to pass. Once God says something, it really is done. Before you see the manifestation of it, it is done. He is in your future, like He was at your beginning and He knows your end and everything in between. So move out of the way! Put the super hero cape back in the closet. Walk with Him, not in front of Him so that you may follow His plan. Enjoy the victory already established in your future. Relax and Breathe. God's got this!

Scripture Meditations: Romans 4, Psalm 46:10, I Corinthians 10:13, Isaiah 43:19

DAY 11: LIVE THE HIGH LIFE

Can you imagine what it is like to be filthy rich and not even know it until you're near the end of your life? Think about it, let's imagine that you lived on a very tight budget all of your life. You made sacrifices, pinched pennies and barely made ends meet to survive. Oh, you were not a pauper, but you seldom experienced the finer things in life—at least not consistently. Now, you are at the very eve of your life and you've just found out that when you were 18 you had legal rights to an unknown inheritance—a large estate that would have changed your life and future generations forever. All you had to do was claim it when you reached age 18 to gain instant access to the funds. If this were true, how might you reflect on your past? What regrets would you have? What would you do differently with the remainder of your life? This is only a hypothetical scenario, but for many believers it is a spiritual reality. We have so much spiritual wealth at our disposal, yet we access so little. There are many wonderfully sweet, saved and faithful people who are living their lives far beneath their potential simply because they don't know their spiritual rights and privileges. You, my friend, were created by God to live the high life.

Understanding what the high life is and living it requires wisdom, knowledge and a paradigm shift in your thinking. As you read today, know that I am praying for you even as the Apostle Paul prayed for God's holy and faithful people at Ephesus,

"For this reason, ever since I heard about your faith in the Lord Jesus and your love for all God's people, I have not stopped giving thanks for you, remembering you in my prayers. I keep asking that the God of our Lord Jesus Christ, the glorious Father, may give you the Spirit of wisdom and revelation, so that you may know him better. I pray that the eyes of your heart may be enlightened in order that you may know the hope to which he has called you, the riches of his glorious inheritance in his holy people, and his incomparably great power for us who believe. That power is the same as

the mighty strength he exerted when he raised Christ from the dead and seated him at his right hand in the heavenly realms, far above all rule and authority, power and dominion, and every name that is invoked, not only in the present age but also in the one to come. And God placed all things under his feet and appointed him to be head over everything for the church, which is his body, the fullness of him who fills everything in every way." Ephesians 1:15-23 (NIV)
Do you understand what that means?

Simplified, in Him you rock! You reign and you rule! It means that in Him, you are powerful! You are supernatural! You are an amazing wonder. Because you are a part of the body of Christ, you are positioned as Jesus is, in heavenly places. You are seated with Jesus, ABOVE ALL, at the right hand of the Father. There is no higher seat. There is no higher place. You reign with him. Have you grasped the revelation of what this really means to your daily life?

When I received the true understanding of my spiritual genetic composite and the reality of God's idea concerning me when He created and redeemed me, it totally changed my life! Everything about me changed. My mind-set, my psyche, my approach to life and even my actions all changed. What's really amazing is that I am still changing. I am constantly moving from faith to faith, from victory to victory, and from glory to glory. Every day, every experience and every situation is new and different. I love it because it's a progressive walk! Grasping this revelation will catapult you to reigning and ruling in this life as you were destined. Don't be deceived. This is far beyond and above just having more money. It is so much greater than that. When you truly grasp this understanding, you will never live another day defeated. You will never accept being depressed. There will be no habit that you cannot break and no victory that you cannot attain. You will live, enjoy and maximize this high life.

Have you ever asked the questions: "Who am I? What am I really made of? What am I here to do?" I will answer those questions for you. There is so much more to you than that meets the eye. You have been made in the image and the likeness of God. Therefore, you have an eternal tripartite nature. That means there are three parts to you and all three parts of you have purpose. I Thessalonians 5:23 lists the three parts to man. It says, "Now may the God of peace make you holy in every way, and may your whole spirit and soul and body be kept blameless until our Lord Jesus Christ comes again." Therefore, you are a **spirit**. You possess a **soul** and You live inside of a **body**. Did you get that? I will say it again so that you can grasp the concept. This time read it slowly. You are really a spirit being. You have a soul and you simply live inside of a body. Unfortunately, in this life of the natural the order has been reversed. Notice the order that is found in I Thessalonians 5:23 the writer is praying that "your spirit (first) -- then your soul and lastly, your body be preserved." Typically, that is not how we refer to ourselves. Often the first emphasis is placed on that which we are most conscious of: body, soul, spirit. Is that not interesting? It is true. For most people, the order is backwards. We must reverse the order in our mindsets and become more conscious of the fact that we are first and foremost spirit beings. We reign and rule in this life through our spirit-man because of Jesus! That's why we can live the high life.

    In order to live the high life you must understand how God created you. He created you to live above this natural realm. Although you are in this world, you are not of this world so the rules of this world should not dictate or control you. The kingdom of God is within you and this kingdom is what is to govern and control you. The real you is neither male nor female. Like God, your spirit is gender neutral yet you have both masculine and feminine sides to your person. You were created to be a god on the earth. You have been placed here, on this earth, as royalty-- to be a king—to reign, rule and to have dominion, to subdue and to replenish the earth! This is God's idea for you. You will maximize your purpose and position when you understand the totality of your person and how you were made to function. You, my friend, are an amazing wonder. And this wonder that you are has nothing to do with your biological parents or generational line. It has nothing to do with the proverbial side of the track you were born on. This has everything to do with your understanding of you and you taking advantage of God's purposes and concepts to reign and rule on this planet earth. You were created to live the high life.

You have got to begin using your words to form your world. As a King, one of your responsibilities is that you make decrees. As a priest, you must execute God's will in the earth. Let's begin this journey into living the high life by confessing some in-Christ realities. Make these confessions a part of your daily walk, and you will begin the process of taking ownership and your rightful place into living the high life.

- I decree that I am in this world but I am not of this world, therefore the rules of this world do not apply to me.
- I decree that I live by a higher government, a higher power and a greater authority!
- I decree that the life of God lives in me. I have His love, his nature and His creative ability.
- I have the creative nature of God living in me therefore I am creating and manifesting what I want to see in my life.
- I decree that I have the mind of Christ! Revelation knowledge & wisdom belongs to me.
- I decree that in Him, I live, move and have my being.
- I decree that I have angelic assistance going before me and working with me today and everyday.
- I decree that I am more than a conqueror through Christ that strengthens me.
- I decree victory belongs to me in every situation because I know no defeat in Him.
- I decree that I am the head and not the tail!
- I decree in every situation, I am favored. I am above and not beneath.

- I decree that neither depression, sickness, nor disease can live in my body. I am the healed of the Lord keeping sickness off of me.
- I decree that I have divine connections and fulfilled relationships.
- I decree no weapon formed against me shall prosper and every tongue that rises up against me in judgment, I shall condemn because that is my right as a servant of God and my righteousness is of Him forever!
- I decree my life, my family and generations to come are saved, well, healed, prosperous, protected and provided for.
- I decree that I will always have more than enough!
- I decree I live in the light of God's word.
- I decree I am obedient to the voice of the Lord that I can clearly hear today!
- I decree today is an awesomely supernatural day. Today I am blessed. Everything I touch is blessed.
- I decree I am free from disbelief, doubt and fear.
- I decree that I live in purpose …on purpose and fulfill my assignment in the earth.
- I decree that I have clear and distinct direction.
- I decree that I have several streams of income and me and my family have limitless wealth, resources, income and power.

Scripture Meditations: I Peter 2:9, Ephesians 1, Rev. 5:10

DAY 12: IT'S A MATTER OF PERSPECTIVE

Life has a way of maximizing our challenges and minimizing our possibilities. We can all identify with bad news, bad circumstances and bad situations that catch us by such surprise, some of which nearly take our breath away! We know what it's like to have more month than money or more problems than solutions. These situations can overwhelm us and leave us feeling helpless, trapped and frustrated. During those times, our perspective is critical. The ability to thrive during these times depends upon one thing, our perception. It's all a matter of perspective! I can almost hear you questioning, "A matter of perspective? It's more like a matter of reality! I really don't have enough resources, money or strength and I really don't know what to do!"

I don't know about you, but I usually manage feelings of frustration and being overwhelmed rather well most of the time. What I typically do not handle quite as well is the thought or feeling of being trapped. I simply cannot stand that feeling. Feeling trapped, for me, tends to open a Pandora's Box of negative issues, feelings, thought patterns and short trips to a place called mental anguish, which truthfully, I simply cannot afford. If I am not careful, feelings of entrapment take me to deep, dark places in my mind from which it becomes quite difficult to escape. Feeling trapped creates an environment for me that says, "There is nothing you can do about where you are. This is your lot, your doomed destiny! It's not ever going to get any better than this!" Talk about misery! Talk about hopelessness! The enemy of our soul knows how much these types of tormenting thoughts paralyze us. That is why he magnifies negative thoughts on the canvas of our minds! He exaggerates challenging situations to cause us to forget who we are and whose we are. If you are a child of God, then you belong to God. God triumphs over evil and the enemy is limited by the amount of power we allow him to exercise over us. Remember, "...greater is He that is in you, than he that is in the world." I John 4:4 (KJV)

Many years ago, I attempted suicide by taking nearly a full

bottle of over the counter pain medication. At the time, I was a college student who worked full time for a ministry. I was a minister of the gospel at the time as well. Life and ministry challenges led me to a place where I felt miserably trapped. I hated my life and I hated where I was in life. Eventually I found myself in a very mentally, emotionally and spiritually abusive place. I decided that if this was all that life had to offer me, I'd much rather take a chance at a better life in the after-life with hopes of being with Jesus. The pressure of life and ministry was too great and the depression was more than I could handle at the time. I felt like there was no way out. I was really afraid of going over the edge. It was becoming harder and harder to resist the pressure and the suggestions to commit suicide that were coming to my mind. I wanted to relieve the pressure. I was angry and wanted to end the cycle of torment, not just so that I could escape the pressure, but I also thought that by removing myself from the situation I could bring peace to others. The only solution that came to mind required me to do some horrible things that would not only disgrace my family, but also bring reproach upon the Kingdom of God. It was all too much. I really loved God and I didn't want to be one of those people who leave a negative legacy and bring reproach upon God or His church.

    My workday ended at 4 pm each day and although I lived just minutes from the church where I worked I drove super slow because I knew in a matter of minutes I would be alone with my thoughts; forced to face the overwhelming gloom and depression. I even purchased dark green blinds for my bedroom window to darken my room during the day so I could sleep as much as possible as a way to avoid dealing with the darkness. I prayed for the Holy Spirit to comfort me and help me sleep believing that as long as I was asleep I could escape the pain. I lived in this torment for nearly three years. When I wasn't working, with friends, or at church, I was very miserable. I felt there was no one to talk to about it except God. I was trapped and losing the will to fight. I recall the disappointment I felt when I realized that I survived the suicide attempt. I said, "Damn! I can't live and I can't die! Why am I here?" During that time my relationship with God was strengthened and I learned invaluable truths that literally saved me from myself. I was still alive and although the situations that led me to this place of despair didn't change immediately, I started to change by allowing God to press the reset button in my mind and change the way I perceived my situation.

The Holy Spirit taught me how to immediately war against feelings of hopelessness and entrapment. I learned that overcoming depression, anxiety, restlessness and feelings of hopelessness hinges upon our ability to change our perspective (how we see ourselves and our situations). I wholeheartedly confess and really believe that I will NEVER be oppressed or depressed another day in my life! Now that's growth! I know that there will be many opportunities to feel depressed, but I choose not to be depressed. It is my choice. Of course there are times when I still cry or feel overwhelmed by life. I still have difficult days; we all do, but I absolutely refuse to wallow in depression and self-pity. There is nothing that happens in my life that God is unaware of or for which He does not have a plan of escape. I choose to trust God to work out every situation, challenge, negative experience, hurt, pain and disappointment in my favor. I choose to trust that He is in control and anything that touches my life is subject to the power of His presence and His Word. When I rely upon God's grace—His ability to do in and through me things I cannot accomplish in my own power, I am able to change my perception and view my challenges as opportunities for victory and not defeat.

I pray today that when you are challenged by depression, lack, fear, etc. that you are able to rise above them and change your perspective. Whenever life presents challenges that seem insurmountable you must live by what you KNOW in your spirit and not what you FEEL with your emotions or what you SEE with your eyes. I've shared my story with you so that you can constantly walk in victory in every situation, every day and in every sphere of your life! So the next time life confronts you by maximizing your challenges and minimizing your possibilities, you too will be able to respond, "It's just a matter of perspective!"

Scripture Meditations: Psalms 112:7, Psalms 34:19, Psalm 23, 2 Corinthians 10:5

DAY 13: JUST SAY, YES!

Imagine what the mother of our Lord stood to lose by choosing to accept the calling of God to be the virgin mother of His only Son. Theologians agree that Mary was somewhere between the ages of 13 and 17 when the angel Gabriel, the messenger of God appeared to her. The angel appeared and said, "Greetings, you who are highly favored! The Lord is with you."

Mary was greatly troubled at his words and wondered what kind of greeting this might be. But the angel said to her, "Do not be afraid, Mary; you have found favor with God. You will conceive and give birth to a son, and you are to call him Jesus. He will be great and will be called the Son of the Most High. The Lord God will give him the throne of his father David, and he will reign over Jacob's descendants forever; his kingdom will never end." "How will this be," Mary asked the angel, "since I am a virgin?" The angel answered, "The Holy Spirit will come on you, and the power of the Most High will overshadow you; so the holy one to be born will be called the Son of God. Even Elizabeth your relative is going to have a child in her old age, and she who was said to be unable to conceive is in her sixth month. For no word from God will ever fail." "I am the Lord's servant," Mary answered. "May your word to me be fulfilled." Then the angel left her.

Mary stood to lose everything. Who would believe her? Would Joseph believe her? He promised to marry her and she's pregnant by the Holy Ghost? Riiiiight. In that day, if a woman was not a virgin at the time of marriage her father's house was shamed. She could be stoned in the streets for not being a virgin at the time of marriage. If she managed to escape that avenue of torture, she was left to fend for herself with only prostitution remaining as means of support.

Consider the beginning of the message from the angel, "The Lord is with you", "Do not be afraid" and "you have found favor with God." Mary could have said, "Is this what favor with God looks like?" But, that's not what she said. Instead, she recognized that this Word from the messenger of God…this encounter and experience would allow her to carry and birth the Living Word! That same Word was destined to change the lives of men forevermore! It was that reality that allowed her to cross the threshold from fear to faith (knowing that God was with her) and bow in humble submission to say, "Yes. I am the Lord's handmaiden. Do whatever you want in me, to me and through me." (Myra Bellinger's Version, LOL) What a place of absolute surrender. What a real and committed Yes!

That is what God is waiting on from you, a real and committed Yes! You have asked to experience His glory at work in your life. You have asked for His favor. He is with you. He requires a yes that has no attachments and no conditions. He wants a yes that is not conditioned upon seeing all of His good promises come to pass in your life. He wants a yes that says, "Even if I lose or suffer some things, I am willing and ready to surrender my life and my plans to Your will." Many years ago, this "Yes" was worked in me. And I must tell you, I have not lived one day to regret it. My Yes, has birthed a level of favor, wisdom and undeniable anointing that rests upon my life. I understand that few people will experience this level of favor in life because they are not willing to pay the price. It is not that God has favorites; it's just that so few are willing to pay the price. What's the price? The same as it was for Mary, a willingness to say Yes and cooperate with the Holy Spirit's plans for your life.

Some years ago, while living in Knoxville, TN, I was dying one more death to self-will. I was in a fight of total surrender of yet another area in my life to the Lord…completely. While in the struggle, I wrote the words of this song:

"There are times in my life, when I just don't understand.
What are you doing Lord? Exactly what's your plan?
It is at those times at best that I travel out so far from your rest.
But, then I know that there is safety in your plan!

Oh yes, I know that there is safety in your plan!
There is safety in your plan. Help me to understand.
Oh yes, I know that there is safety in your plan.
So, help me to surrender my will and way to you.
Help me to surrender Lord, only you know what I should do.
Help me to surrender Lord, and help me to obey.
Help me to say yes and just learn how to wait.
Because I know that there is safety in your plan."

God has a plan for your life! He just needs your cooperation. He's a perfect gentleman, who has given you free moral agency. That means He has given you the power and right to make choices in life. He wants you to choose His way and His plans for your life. He knows everything about you, better than you know yourself. Saying Yes to Him is an easy task when we view it from the perspective of knowing God's plan for your life is good. He promised, "I know the thoughts that I have towards you. They are thoughts of peace and not of evil to give you a hope and a future." Jeremiah 29:11 (NIV) Say yes! You'll be glad you did!

Scripture Meditations: St. Luke 1:26-38, John 2:5, I Samuel 15:22, Isaiah 1:19, Philippians 2:13

DAY 14: POSTURE FOR A MIRACLE

When life's challenges come from seemingly every side, we throw our hands up and cry out, "Lord, please help! I need a miracle!" However, is a miracle what we REALLY need? Granted, I am certain that in some cases nothing short of a miracle will do! In other cases however, a good old dose of the six-fold concoction of expectation, faith, perseverance, plus stand-a-ability, stick-to-itiveness & time will bring about the desired result.

What is a miracle? "Bakers Dictionary of the Bible defines a miracle as 'an event in the external world brought by the immediate agency or the simple volition of God.' It goes on to add that a miracle occurs to show that the power behind it is not limited to the laws of matter as it interrupts fixed natural laws. So the term supernatural applies quite accurately."[1] I like to say it this way, **a miracle is divine intervention in the ordinary course of nature.** Miracles are nothing short of the signature of God. They are acts that only He can perform exclusively and without the help of man. In fact, the performance of a miracle has nothing to do with the ability of man and often defies or supersedes the basic laws of nature. An article entitled, <u>Miracles of the Bible</u> suggests there are two basic types of miracles that we see in the Word of God. There are miracles of creation (which supersedes the basic laws of nature) and miracles of providence (which operates within the laws but which manipulate the timing, location or rate of natural processes).[2]

There are many miracles found in scripture. A few of the miracles of creation are: The creation of the worlds and mankind, the unconsumed burning bush, feeding of the five thousand and the many miracles of healing and "raising up of people," in both the Old

---
[1] http://www.probe.org/site/c.fdKEIMNsEoG/b.4222629/k.EE2A/What_is_a_Biblical_Definition_of_Miracle.htm
[2] http://www.bbcmorehead.org/

and New Testament are found in this category. Some examples of the miracles of providence are the plagues and the winds sent by God to Egypt, the stilling of the waves, Elijah's three and one half year drought, the opening of prison doors and the release of Peter from prison.

We understand that we cannot perform a miracle, but the reality is sometimes we really do need a miracle. In some situations, if our God does not intervene… Need I say more? I am thankful that when I need a miracle, I do not have to wait to be next in line! Neither do I have to wait for my turn while others go before me. I am grateful that a season does not depict when I will receive my miracle from God. God is still in the miracle working business and He is faithful today to meet me at the point of my need! When His children are really in need of divine intervention, He knows how and when to intervene.

So, what do you do when you really need a miracle from God? In Mark's Gospel chapter 5 verses 25-34, there is a "certain woman," who demonstrates the proper posture to take when we are in need of a miracle. From these nine verses of scripture, we glean a massive amount of revelation. There are seven main points to consider from this text.

Now a 'certain woman' had a flow of blood for twelve years, and had suffered many things from many physicians. She had spent all that she had and was no better, but rather grew worse. When she heard about Jesus, she came behind Him in the crowd and touched His garment. For she said, "If only I may touch His clothes, I shall be made well." Immediately the fountain of her blood was dried up, and she felt in her body that she was healed of the affliction. And Jesus, immediately knowing in Himself that power had gone out of Him, turned around in the crowd and said, "Who touched My clothes?" But His disciples said to Him, "You see the multitude thronging You, and You say, 'Who touched Me?'" And He looked around to see her who had done this thing. But the woman, fearing and trembling, knowing what had happened to her, came and fell down before Him and told Him the whole truth. And He said to her, "Daughter, your faith has made you well. Go in peace, and be healed of your affliction."

Pay attention to the underlined instructions as revealed in the text.
- The bible depicts her as "a certain woman." Notice, <u>her name was insignificant</u>. Where she came from, her family background or what she did occupationally did not seem to matter. Her "issue" or <u>her "need" was the focus</u> of the text!

- Notice that not only had her issue been around for a long time, but <u>she also exhausted ALL of HER own resources</u>. She did EVERYTHING she knew to do to solve the problem. She came to the end of herself, her natural resources and her ability to fix her situation. In the vernacular of my Williams Family cousins, SHE WAS FLAT!

- <u>No one around her, who should have been able to help, could help her</u>. They too, did what they could do and to no avail! Even with all of their help, she only grew worse!

- <u>SHE HEARD</u> someone else's testimony <u>about the goodness and miracle working power of</u> Jesus! She obviously concluded that if he could do it for them, His power would work for her too! Faith comes by hearing and hearing <u>the Word of God</u>. Hearing those testimonies persuaded her that if she could just get to Him, her situation (issue/need) would be gone forever!

- <u>SHE PRESSED</u> because she heard. Her faith gave her the strength to disregard her condition, her own abilities (or lack thereof), and the opinion of others. The custom of the day dictated that she should have stayed home or at least stay away from people because of her issue. But <u>she paid no attention to what others thought or said about her</u>. She closed everyone and everything else out and pressed into the

61

crowd to get to the only one who could solve her problem.

- The Bible says, <u>FOR SHE SAID,</u> "If only I may touch His clothes, I shall be made well." In the original text, "for" is translated "because." Notice closely, the order of the text. She got the guts and stamina to come behind Him to touch Him only AFTER she heard. After she heard, <u>SHE DECREED the outcome</u>. Her situation was desperate, but faith arose causing her to make a bold prophetic proclamation! "I shall be whole, if only I can touch!

- <u>SHE TOUCHED</u>. In a sermon, my husband, Pastor Gary Bellinger made a simple observation that made me see this text a bit differently. Why was her decree limited to touching the hem of His garment? Could it have been because of what she heard about the hem or all of the spiritual connotations of the hem? Did she hear anything at all about it? Or, was it because she really was "flat," as in bowed over or nearly helpless or maybe even prostrate on the ground because of twelve years of non-stop bleeding? Perhaps she really had no strength to stand up or walk around like normal people. In either case, <u>it was the faith in her prophetic declaration that determined her outcome</u>. Notice, <u>her miracle had nothing to do with Jesus' faith</u>. He did not initiate it. He did not know she was in need. He did not even know who she was. It was her actions and her posture that gave her the miracle she needed.

So, the next time you are in need of a miracle my friend, learn from this certain woman how to receive your miracle from God! To receive your miracle, hear the Word, press through the obstacles, prophetically decree (speak) your outcome and then touch God with your need.

Scripture Meditations: Mark 5:25-34, Romans 10:17, Job 22:8, Matt. 21:22

BELIEVE

DAY 15: SHINE YOUR LIGHT ON ME

When I was growing up in church, there was an old song that we sang, 'Shine on Me.' The words of the song said, "Shine on me. Shine on me. Let the light from the lighthouse shine on me." I liked that song. I felt good when I sang that song. Sometimes, I would even worship God with my tears as I sang it. That song was deep in meaning to me although the words are so simple. My spirit identified with the song as a prayer, but I did not really have a clue of the true depth of the song. As I grew older, I began to understand exactly what the song (prayer) meant.

Lighthouses have always had two principal functions: to warn of danger and to be guides.[3] The lighthouse in the song represents God, all that He is, and all that He does. He is God and He is good—not only is He good to me, He is good for me! His Holy Spirit is in the earth today to lead and guide me into all truth. He is here to bring direction and peace. He alerts me of impending danger, even when the potential danger is because of a choice or a decision I made. He provides hope in darkness and provides safety for all of my transitions and travels. He aids, assists, instructs, and corrects.

The "Light" that comes from the "Lighthouse" is the Word of God. Psalms 119:105 says, "Your word is a lamp to my feet. And a light to my path." That answers some of our common life questions like, "How can I have safety? How can I have direction? How can I know the right way to go?" The answer is clear. Everything you need is in the Word of God. As we learn about God, we find that He is consistent with His Word. That means He never leads or directs outside of the parameters of His word. His word and His will are one!

We have clarity on the "Light" and the "Lighthouse," but there is one more character in the song that we must give attention

---

[3] (http://americanhistory.si.edu/collections/lighthouses/history.htm)

to—me. The song says, "Let the Light from the Lighthouse shine on ME." The song that my Spirit so identified with is really a desperate request to God from my core, my innermost being, to please help me, shine on me and show me. As I sang the song, I wanted God to shine on me, but I also gave the Holy Spirit permission to save me from myself. I gave Him the right to come in and do what He is commissioned to do in the earth. He comes to make everything right within us. As I ask the Light to shine on me, I recognize that when He shines the Light, darkness flees and confusion is eradicated!

As He shines the Light, I must to be willing to expose myself, my entire self to the Light. As He gives light (direction, instruction, correction etc.) to me, I cannot choose to close my eyes and ears to the light. I cannot choose where I want the Light to shine; but I must cooperate with Him and know that the light of Jesus will expose bad, hurting or injured things within me. The Light has the capacity in itself to heal every dark part of my soul!

So, if you are bold enough to pray this prayer with me or to sing the song, "Let the light from the Lighthouse shine on me," know that the Light comes to show you, you! He exposes the root issues in your life that have hindered you. He gives you answers to problems, but you must be willing to cooperate with him. Many people spend their lives nursing and treating symptoms only. Rarely, do they dig and find the root. Rarely do they know or understand the "why" behind their actions or feelings. Many things that we do are just the fruit off the tree, but it is not the root. The Light of Jesus will expose roots—the why.

The song that my Spirit identified with as a young girl, was a request to God from the city of my soul, to please help me, shine on me and show me myself; and then save me from myself. If you ask the Light from the Lighthouse to shine on you, then use the Light. Find scriptures in the Bible that correspond to your need or request and then follow His instructions.

Scripture Meditations: Psalm 139, John 1:12, Proverbs 3:5-6, Malachi 4:2, Jeremiah 17:14

DAY 16: THE FORCE IS WITH YOU

In the world of Star Wars, the phrase "May the force be with you." is a phrase first used as a formal "goodbye" and "good luck" among Jedi. Generally, when they part ways or the object of the expression was facing some sort of imminent danger, the phrase implied the speaker's wish that the power of the Force would be working alongside the person to effectively accomplish their goals. The members of the Jedi High Council often recited it after assigning missions to their Jedi Knights.

An unseen force and power assists us in accomplishing our purposes. Yes, the force is with you! I am not trying to spook you or be mystical, but there is more to life than what meets the eye! There is a world more real, permanent and powerful than the one in which we live. There is a spirit world that we cannot physically see. Hebrews 11:3 says, "Through faith we understand that the worlds were framed by the word of God, so that things which are seen were not made of things which do appear." Angels exist in this unseen world. Angels are God's special messengers to and for us. Throughout scripture, we see the presence of angels at work. They gave simple directions to God's people to fulfill their purposes since early Bible days. (II Kings 1:3, Acts 5:19, Acts 8:26, Acts 10:5).

The most incredible thing is that angels not only existed in the stories we have read in the Bible, but angels are assigned to us today! Hebrews 1:14 says, "What are all the angels? They are spirits sent to serve those who are going to receive salvation." (God's Word Translation) The King James Version of this scripture says, "Are they not all ministering spirits, sent forth to minister for them who shall be heirs of salvation?" Do you understand what this scripture is saying to you? Angles are present today to serve and assist you in your earthly purpose. We each have angels assigned to us. You may ask, "What will my angel help me do?"

According to Matthew 18:10, your angel has been with you since childhood! "See that you do not despise one of these little ones.

For I tell you that their angels in heaven always see the face of my Father in heaven." According to Psalm 34:7, your angel is present for deliverance and protection! "The angel of the LORD encamps around those who fear him, and he delivers them." According to Psalm 91:11-12, your angel is there to guide you, lift you up and ensure your safety! "For he will command his angels concerning you to guard you in all your ways; they will lift you up in their hands so that you will not strike your foot against a stone." Hebrews 13:2 even suggests that we may have seen and spoken with an angel face to face! "Do not forget to show hospitality to strangers, for by so doing some people have shown hospitality to angels without knowing it."

That is just a few of the things that your angels are doing for you. So as you go through today and every day, know that a powerful force goes with and works for you. I pray that the next time you feel like you are the underdog, your back is against the wall or you do not have help, the Lord will open your eyes to see there are more with you than there are against you. May you see and know that the 'force' is with you.

Scripture Meditation: II Kings 6

DAY 17: I WILL NEVER MAKE YOU ASHAMED

As I sat in the car waiting for my daughter to finish her theater class, as clear as day, I heard, "**I may not say everything you'd like; but I will never make you ashamed.**" This phrase not only made me smile, but it brought back memories I cannot even begin to write about. You see, my great great-grandmother, Dr. E.V. Ervin coined that phrase. It was one of her mottos in life. She was a Bishop in her reformation. Wherever she served and in each jurisdiction, this was one of two phrases she was known for quoting.

To my understanding, she was an awesome counselor, teacher and stern administrator. I did not know her in all of those capacities. I do remember traveling a lot with her in ministry, her sense of humor, her love for great food and yes, her sayings; but most of all I remember her most affectionately as my Granny! I gained a lot of wisdom from my Granny, and yes, as I have grown I have taken on that motto too. That saying is true when there is a call of leadership on your life—in any capacity. Leaders are positioned with purpose. Sometimes you must say hard things, motivated by love of course. Depending upon the season and the assignment, you may not be the most liked person in the bunch. You must find within yourself, the wisdom of God and hold true to your assignment.

As I sat in the car reflecting on this statement that made me think of my Granny, it was not the memories of Granny speaking to me at all. The words were actually in present tense from the Lord to me. I knew at that very moment He was communicating with me. It was totally unsolicited. I was not thinking about Granny, the phrase, or God at that moment. It was as if He just decided to strike up a conversation with me. Has that ever happened to you? He used my Granny's words to convey His heart to me. He was telling me what page He was on in the moment. Having a relationship with the Lord is so awesome! You do not have to be bowed down in prayer or on some long fast, starving yourself to hear Him communicate with you. He wants open and natural communication between the two of you.

God communicated with me that day in the car the way it is with Him and His word. "I may not say everything you like, but I'll never make you ashamed." Often, when we read His word we feel blessed, encouraged, strengthened and helped. Sometimes when we hear some things from His word, it is the extreme opposite. It does not feel so good because it goes directly against what we may want to do or what we may want to hear. Sometimes His word comes to harness, correct and constrain us. His word comes to instruct and lead us, to follow His way—the path of righteousness, not our way—the path of destruction.

Honestly, I can think of a number of times while reading the word of God or just following His leading, I got slightly upset. I could not believe that God would require such a thing of me! I experienced times when I thought the Word and His direction was either too harsh or too unfair. I did not want to agree. Of course, I thought and felt those things in my flesh. In my spirit, I knew it was the Word of the Lord to me and I had no other choice but to obey or be ashamed. My spirit agreed and in those moments, I chose to do what I knew was right, not what felt good to me! Does that make sense to you? Remember, man is a spirit that possesses a soul and lives on the inside of a body. In order to follow God more fully, we must realize that feeling is the voice of the body. Reason is the voice of the mind and conscience is the voice of the spirit. To live a life totally free of shame, we must trust, receive and obey the Word of the Lord...no matter how it makes us feel, fully assured that He knows all and always has our best interests at heart! When we do, we will never be ashamed. In the words of the old hymn, "Trust and obey for there's no other way to be happy in Jesus, but to trust and obey." He will NEVER make you ashamed!

Scripture Meditations: John 6:63, Psalms 119:165, Hebrews 4:12

DAY 18: THE CONTRADICTION OF YOUR FAITH

Have you ever had a season of ease, relaxation and seemingly no worries, like a summer season? Perhaps you have experienced seasons of mountain top experiences in life, where it seems everything was wonderful (maybe not perfect, but things were good with you and God). Maybe you have had a season wherein everything you touched turned to gold or in which there was an abundance of good things happening at once, like love, life, family, peace and money. Then...

Have you ever tried to believe God for something during a season of good things happening and it was easy? There was a time that you had innocent child-like faith and could believe God for you and for others. A season when you grabbed a hold onto the altar and were able to pray through on someone else's behalf? Maybe you can relate to a season wherein you felt like you had done everything right with God and He was pleased with you. You knew it and your faith level was oh sooo good. And then...

BAM! The seasons changed and OMG what a change! You entered a time of great trial, tribulation, frustration and distress. Did it seem like nothing worked in your life? A time when everything was hard, the ground dried up & nothing grew? Maybe you've never experienced such a season in your faith wherein it felt like you couldn't even believe God for a Hershey bar, and definitely not to pay a bill, or for healing, or deliverance. Well, you *"tried"* to believe. You did all the right things and made all the right confessions but it just did not seem to work. Well my friend, I have come to let you know today that you are no different from any other person of faith INCLUDING Jesus. You are simply in a season of the contradiction of your faith.

What is a contradiction? A contradiction is a direct opposition between things compared or inconsistency. What might the contradiction of your faith look like? Here are some practical possibilities. You are experiencing the contradiction of your faith when:

- You are confessing and giving and by your own standard, you are faithful to God, His church, His Word (sowing on every wave, giving your tithe and offerings), and STILL out of nowhere comes expenses and bills; unpleasant unexpected mail that does not bring good news when you already didn't have enough to start with and you suddenly need more...and you have more bills and needs than money.... (I know it is a run-on statement, but that is exactly what that moment feels like—one long 'run-on' season of frustration.)

- You are eating right, exercising and trying to take good care of the temple and you are well disciplined at it. You get up and make daily confessions over your body and then out of nowhere, while going for a routine checkup, you get a bad report from the doctor that shakes your world.

- When you raised your children to the best of your knowledge and ability in the fear and admonition of the Lord, been a good example before them, kept them in church and you wake up one day to find out they have begun making choices and doing things that are so far from everything, you have ever taught them.

- You are in the will of God and you still find yourself going through and looking crazy, in derision daily like Jeremiah. Jeremiah did everything God told him to do—no matter how crazy it seemed or looked, yet he was a laughingstock to all. It made him so angry, that he did not want to speak for God anymore, but he had no other choice. He understood if he did not, the word would be like fire shut up in his bones.

In the season of the contradiction of your faith, all that matters is WHAT GOD TOLD YOU. Circumstances and situations may not line up, but that still does not change what God has said. Here are some steps to help you through the season of the contradiction of your faith:

- Recognize that if you are walking with God, doing things his way that this is just a season. So get the lessons from the season. Understand the wisdom given and the purposes revealed. (Eccl. 3:1)

- Get on With it. Run the race that is set before you. Do not be afraid to strip down, lay aside every weight and sin, so that you can run this race with ease.

- Never Quit. You must decide that quitting is not an option! Stay consistent and faithful to what God is saying to you, even when circumstances and situations change.

- DO NOT CHANGE YOUR POSITIVE OUTLOOK NOR YOUR CONFESSION!

- Keep Your Eyes on Jesus—understanding & studying how He did everything according to Hebrews 12: 1-3. (The Message Bible)

"Do you see what this means—all these pioneers who blazed the way, all these veterans cheering us on? It means we had better get on with it. Strip down, start running—and never quit! No extra spiritual fat, no parasitic sins. Keep your eyes on Jesus, who both began and finished this race. Study how he did it. He never lost sight of where he was headed—that exhilarating finish in God and with God. He put up with every obstacle along the way. Now He is there, in the place of honor, right alongside God. When you find yourselves flagging in your faith, go over that story again, item by item, that long litany of hostility He plowed through to get to the place of faith. That will shoot adrenaline into your souls! In this all-out match against sin, others have suffered far worse than you have, to say nothing of what Jesus went through—all that bloodshed! So do not feel sorry for yourselves. Or, have you forgotten how good parents treat their children and that God regards you as his child?"

Jesus never lost sight of where he was heading. He knew victory was at the end. Now look at him! He remained in contact with the Father. Sometimes you just have to go back to the Father and say, "Tell me again Father what you are saying about me? Please Lord, show me, breathe in me again!" Remember, your praise, worship and prayer life are IMPERATIVE. DO NOT let the enemy fool or distract you. Jesus understood His purpose & worked it. Jesus knew the Word. He studied the Word. He lived the Word and He spoke the Word only.

Come on. Endure the season of the contradiction of your faith by focusing on the joy that is set before you! YOU ARE AN OVERCOMER AND A WINNER IN EVERY SITUATION!

Scripture Meditations: Ecclesiastes 3, I Corinthians 9:24-27, Hebrews 12, Philippians 3:13-14

DAY 19: STOP WORRYING

An ancient adage says, "If you want to defeat them, distract them." Whether we like it or not, whether we are comfortable with the terminology or not, Satan is the god of this world and this worlds' system. One of the greatest weapons that he uses against God's people is distraction. He uses the cares of this world to keep us out of balance and out of focus. When we become so burdened about things that we cannot change, how we will make ends meet, or what we need, we begin to worry. When we worry, fear is eminent. To worry is to afflict with mental distress or agitation: make anxious. The enemy is always trying to keep us distressed so we will stay in a place of agitation. If we stay in that place of agitation, it is impossible for us to be productive and time is lost. Time is a precious commodity. Do not spend your time and energy worrying because once time is spent you can never get it back.

Jesus was in the middle of his sermon on the mount when He changed his focus and began to address the issue of worrying. He said,

> Therefore do not worry, saying, 'What shall we eat?' or 'What shall we drink?' or 'What shall we wear?' For after all these things the Gentiles seek. For your Heavenly Father knows that you need all these things. But seek first the kingdom of God and His righteousness, and all these things shall be added to you. Therefore, do not worry about tomorrow, for tomorrow will worry about its own things. Sufficient for the day *is* its own trouble. Matthew 6:31-33 (NKJV)

There you have it! That is Jesus' remedy for worrying today. Just in case you missed it, here is what He said. These are Jesus' instructions for a worry-free life:

- Decide to stop worrying about things you need (what you are going to eat, drink or wear). Why? Only sinners need to worry!

- Meditate on the reality that God already knows EVERYTHING you need...even before you knew you needed it.

- Use your energy instead to please him! Focus all of your attention on doing things His way.

Then just sit back and watch how your loving, all-knowing Heavenly Father supplies all of your needs.

Scripture Meditations: Philippians 4:19, St. Mark 4:13-20, St. Matthew 6:31-33

DAY 20: SEE "LOVE" RIGHT

Love is a very popular word. It is a basic need for all life. Although 'love' is a popular word, few understand its meaning. What is love, really? It's certainly not what most people think that it is. It's definitely not a feeling. It's definitely not inconsistent. It never hurts on purpose. It is not short-lived and is not easily provoked. The reality is that it is difficult for us to fully understand and thoroughly grasp what love really is and the real power or force behind it.

It is so hard for us to comprehend this reality because we are human and we spend most of our time dealing with other humans. Our definition of love is usually based on our experiences with people. However, people cannot show us true love. A person may love us, but their love usually comes with conditions. When we fail to meet the conditions of their love they withdraw, flip the script or change the way they express their love towards us. The love people offer one another often says, "As long as my feelings are warm and fuzzy towards you I will love you, and I will support you, and I will accept you. I will be consistent with you and continue to show you my love and approval." And I say, ALL OF THAT IS WRONG!

Love is a basic necessity for life. But my friend, real love is what we all need. So what is real love? Love is God and God is Love! I know that you may have heard that before, but do you really grasp what that means? God is the personification of love. Love is His very essence. That means love is what He is made of. So nothing evil or shady can come from Him or out of Him. When you see love right, you understand that even if you don't get it all right today or tomorrow or any other day, God still loves you. God still cares for you and He is still committed to you. He desires the very best for you. When you see love right, you understand that His love is not predicated upon your actions, but upon His Person and His decision to love you.

You see, He is perfect. His love is perfect towards us even when we are not. He accepts you and me even when our ways are less than perfect. We are already accepted in the Beloved! (Ephesians 1:6) That means just as I am, far from the finished product I know I am going to be, He has accepted me. He is still committed to me right now! Right in the midst of my imperfection, His love is perfect towards me. God's love for us is not that funny love based on feelings or how well we perform. Even when we mess up, He is still working in us to get us to the expected end that He has for us. And His thoughts towards us are always good. He has great plans for you! His plans are His will and His predestined desire and purpose for us. He has promised, "I know the plans that I have for you, declares the LORD. They are plans for peace and not disaster plans to give you a future filled with hope." Jeremiah 29:11 (GW)

Love is the most powerful force in the universe. It is powerful enough to change any situation. I know it is hard to believe that someone as great, as powerful and as perfect as God could, would and does love us unconditionally, but He does! You are the apple of His eye! (Psalm 17:8) Embrace His all encompassing, consistent love today!

Scripture Meditation: I Corinthians 13 (AMP)

DAY 21: DON'T LIVE IN FEAR OF MISSING GOD

Fear is a small four-letter word that potentially has devastating effects. Fear can result in massive destruction. Fear is a distressing emotion aroused by impending danger, evil, pain, etc., whether the threat is real or imagined. It is the feeling or condition of being afraid. Have you ever been negatively impacted by the **spirit of fear**? It is easy for the spirit of fear to grip you after you have made several costly mistakes or repeated poor choices. If you are not careful, you will be so gripped by fear that you become immobilized and unable to make any choices or decisions.

God does not want us paralyzed with fear when making choices and decisions. He does not want us to be afraid to make a move or take a risk. He does not want us living in fear of 'missing' His direction. He also does not want us to continue to make poor choices and bad decisions. God is progressive and He wants his children to be progressive—living and moving by faith, not fear. Fear causes us to be apathetic rather than kinetic—with fast-paced energy and movement. Faith is an action word. It requires that we "do something!" We cannot be afraid to make decisions. When we allow fear to control our willingness to make decisions, we live in fear and not faith.

Many years ago, I came to a junction in my life where I had to make a very serious decision. This decision was what I believe to have been the most important decision of my life up to that time. I was single and in full time ministry. God and I were in a great place. I felt He was pleased with me and I was totally pleased with Him. I was living my life to the fullest, enjoying every moment of it and following His instructions to the best of my ability. I was happy. I was satisfied. I was fulfilled. Then seemingly, almost out of nowhere, comes this man by the name of Gary Bellinger with 'his word' from the Lord that said I was to be his wife. Imagine that. Really??? It really took the wisdom of God and the knowledge of the Holy Spirit to help me be open to God in that moment and receive His direction for my life; or else I would have lost my natural mind and definitely my faith in my ability to hear from God.

It was not Gary's "word from the Lord" that challenged me. I have heard that same word from other people before. I have learned to live by the premise that it is not enough for someone else to hear a "word from the Lord" for me. I need to hear a "word from the Lord" for myself. After all, God lives in me and He communicates with me daily. This is a sidebar, but if someone has a 'word from the Lord' that does not bear witness with what you already know, or if it is new information to you, one of two things is occurring: 1) It is false or 2) Something is short-circuiting your ability to hear what God is communicating to you. He communicates with every individual. You must choose to tune into His frequency to hear Him.

Let's get back to my story. Again, it was not Gary's word that challenged me; it is what began to happen on the inside of me that challenged me. The possibility of him being my husband went against EVERYTHING I believed to be true up to that point. Until this time, for nearly 3 years, I thought I knew who I would marry. I journaled events, dreams, details and words that confirmed my belief. I was not a desperate girl. Gary was not my type—naturally or spiritually at the time. I even told him, when he got up the nerve to tell me what God said to him, "Well, I am so sorry. That is not what God told me!" I was not trying to be mean. I said it as nice as I possibly could, but that was my reality. It was my belief system. So how did we end up married six weeks later? Something began to happen on the inside of me that forced me to seek God in a desperate sort of way. I mean I REALLY had to seek God.

I was desperate for His direction and I was now feeling confused and afraid. I was determined not to miss God in this. This was way too crazy, but also way too important to make the wrong decision. This one decision would impact and potentially affect everything about my life, including the most important thing in my life, which was ministry. Ministry, for me, means being in the complete and total will of God. It is beyond preaching a sermon or pastoring a church. Many people live miserable and hindered lives because they did not marry 'God's choice' for them. While this entry is not about choosing the right mate, I do want to clarify my perspective. I do not believe God chooses your mate. I do believe however, that He presents choices and you choose. Back to my desperate need to seek God…

    I felt the need to go on a shut-in. I call a shut-in a time of shutting out the world, other voices and distractions to focus on the discipline of silence and communication with God. I needed to know what was really going on inside. Why was I suddenly questioning what I knew to be true? How could this person, whom I knew nothing about, come and change everything that I hoped, expected and believed to be true for so long? My soul and my spirit were wrestling for peace, understanding and truth. I had other options. So again, I was NOT desperate to be married. The saying is, "To thine own self be true." I knew something was going on inside of me. I know how God leads me. I know when He is directing me. I know when He is trying to communicate something to me and He was definitely trying to communicate about this. It was the Lord that sent the "rumble," or the "alert to my spirit that required me to tune into the frequency that He was now on for my life.

    For several days, the singer, Yolanda Adams' "Open Up My Heart" spoke volumes to me. The words, "Lord, I need to talk to you and ask you for your guidance, especially today when my life is so cloudy. Guide me until I'm sure. I open up my heart to you," resounded within me. I literally listened and prayed that song for hours a day. I actually did not have a whole lot of other deep things to say. But, I did say things like, "God, please help me. Don't let me be deceived. Please cover me. Please direct me. Please Father, I can't miss you!" I was in an almost desperate agony.

    During the shut-in one night, while lying in bed, I drifted off to sleep. Awakened by the sound of my own spirit singing to me the sentiments of my heart to God. I asked God to help me. I heard the song, "Order my steps in your word Dear Lord. Lead me. Guide me every day. Send your anointing, Father I pray. Order my steps in your word! PLEASE order my steps in your word!" I cannot begin to describe how afraid I was of making the wrong decision and totally missing out on the will of God for my life! I suddenly had the urge to go into the bathroom. I still heard the song playing on the inside. I know that might sound strange, but it was so loud. It was my own voice singing and nearly begging God. "I want to walk worthy! Please order my steps." As I crossed the threshold to enter the bathroom, the song changed from my voice to another voice. I then begin to hear, "The steps of a good man are ordered by the Lord and He delighteth in his way! (Psalms 37:23)" Then back to the song. Then back to the other voice. I recognized that using these two messages God was communicating something to me, but I did not yet understand the meaning of the message, although I understood the words I heard so clearly.

  I asked God to please make it plain so I could understand what He was saying. Suddenly, I intuitively understood what God was communicating to me. In this time of seeking Him, my belief system was not changed but the foundation of my belief system was strengthened and clarified to me. I knew in that moment that God was saying to me, "I have instructed you to acknowledge me in all your ways and you do. You have asked me to direct your path and I will! Remember, that is my promise to you. Myra, you are not like most! Most people don't ask or acknowledge, but because your heart is God-ward and you want to please me. Do you think I would let you miss me? And even if by some chance or somehow you did miss me, Myra, I'd find you, because I am God!" Wow! Talk about a burden lifted! Talk about the spirit of fear leaping off of me! Talk about being relieved of distress and agony! I was free from the fear of decision making in an instant and I have never been the same since that very moment. I no longer agonize about making the wrong choices or decisions. I simply tune into His frequency, make sure my motives are right and trust God!

Let's consider a story from scripture and a lesson we can learn from the life of Peter. According to Matthew, Chapter 14, the will of God for Peter was to "get in the boat with the others and go to the other side." At some point as they were in the boat, Peter sees Jesus walking on the water. Now, he is not certain that this is Jesus that he sees. But he says to whom he sees, "Master, if it is you, bid me to come!" Now it was Jesus, who could not deny that he was himself. So he responds to Peter, "Come." So, Peter begins to walk on the water to Jesus. Remember, the will of God was for Peter to get in the boat and go to the other side. I don't know why Peter requested to come to Jesus on the water. Perhaps he was afraid. Perhaps he was excited to see Jesus. Perhaps he wanted to do what Jesus was doing. Whatever the reason, the initial instruction from the Lord (God's will) was for Peter to get in the boat and go to the other side. As Peter walked on the water with Jesus, the waves and the wind got turbulent and Peter began to sink. As Peter sinks, Jesus picks him up and leads him back into the boat! Is that not amazing? Jesus simply helped Peter despite the position Peter put Jesus in to respond to his question. I have heard this passage preached a number of times and a number of ways. Most of the time the text is preached from a view that shows that Peter had little faith and became distracted by the wind and the waves. And while Jesus did comment on Peters' 'little faith', I choose to believe that this passage also shows Peter's great faith, because who can actually walk on water, with or without distractions? I also believe that this passage is more about us seeing the caring, protecting and loving nature of our Lord, who instructs, helps, directs and redirects us at any and every point in our lives.

You too can experience the freedom both Peter and I discovered when making choices and decisions. You do not have to fear that you might miss God. The key to making right choices and decisions is that your heart is God-ward. That means you want what He wants for you, and you desire to please Him in all of your ways. He is obligated to direct your path when this is your posture!

Scripture Meditations: Job 32:8, Proverbs 16:3 (Amplified), Matthew 14:22-32

DAY 22: YOU CAN KNOW HIS WILL

It is amazing how many people are bamboozled to think that they can never know the will of God for their lives. Conceptually, they find it hard to believe that they can know something so deep about themselves. As a result, they spend their lives guessing, hoping, wishing and praying they are able to figure it out. All the while, they make bad choices and decisions that are costly, painful and time consuming. I want to dispel the myth that it is impossible to know God's will for your life. God does not want us to live our lives like a crapshoot, accepting anything that the roll of the die gives us. He wants us to live with purpose on purpose. He wants us to know His will.

Ephesians 5:17 [Amplified] says, "Therefore do not be vague *and* thoughtless *and* foolish, but understanding *and* firmly grasping what the will of the Lord is." We should not only 'know' His will, but we should firmly grasp and understand His will. What then, is the will of God? God's will is His ways, His purposes, His plans, and His desires. We find all of these things through the study of His Word and through spending time with Him. It is important to understand that His will and His word are one. They will always agree. Knowing the will of God requires us to develop a relationship with Him. When we do, we begin to learn His likes and dislikes. We begin to comprehend how He communicates with us. It is most important to be sensitive to the sound of His voice and develop an ear to hear when He is speaking. One way to know you are on the right track and accurately understanding Him is to know that He will always direct you in line with His Word. That means He will never instruct you to do something that is contrary to what is written in His word. The simplest way to think of it is ask yourself the question, "How do I know when someone is communicating something with me even when they're not using their words? How do I know what they are thinking or feeling?" Typically, when you develop a close relationship with someone, words are optional in communication. You learn so much about each other until you understand each other, even without words. It's the same way with God.

    I too sought God about how I can know and understand His will for my life. When I talk to God, I am not "spooky", super-holy, or extra deep. I talk to Him just like I am talking to a friend. I told Him I needed to know His direction and His ways for my life. I told Him how desperately I wanted to know His will because I didn't trust myself to know what is best for me. At some point in my life, I began to understand and became fully persuaded that God really is my best, constant and only immutable friend. As I am typing this entry at this very moment, I am chuckling. I just had a flashback. I can actually remember when I learned the word "immutable." I was sitting in a church service. I actually heard what was like a man whisper in my ear and I knew it was the Lord. He said, "I am the ONLY immutable one in your life!" I was so moved by the experience, I hurried to find the definition of the word. Immutable means incapable of changing! This promise was extra wonderful to me because I was in a season of tremendous hurt, pain and close disillusionment. I experienced the pain of disappointment and abuse by someone with whom I had a divine relationship, a God-given present. However, the relationship became polluted. I did not understand how wrong things were happening to something that was designed to be so right! It was in this season that I learned that I didn't need 66 books of scripture memorized. I just needed an open heart and a willingness to trust God. It's funny sometimes how desperate, painful and barren seasons will fine-tune your hearing. God does not make understanding His will for your life a difficult quest. It is not hidden to them who pursue it. God waits on us to invite Him into our affairs and allow Him to take control of the reigns. It's a simple process. Just tell Him that you want Him to take control. "Jesus, take the wheel!" Tell Him you want His will for your life. Then step back and allow Him to do it. In this season I found this promise in Psalms 32:8 (KJV) that encouraged me. It says, "I will instruct you and teach you in the way you should go; I will guide you with My eye." I also learned, "that it is better to trust in the Lord than to put confidence in man." Because, "cursed in the man that trusts in man and makes flesh His arm!" (Psalm 118:8, Jeremiah 17:5)

    God loves you and has your best interest at heart. I am certain that He is the only one that really knows everything that is best for me. Not only is He my friend, but He is my creator. Only the creator of a thing knows its intended purpose. God created me and He actually had a purpose in mind when He did. I trust Him more than anyone; including myself. He wants me to know His will. People have asked me how I got to this place of trust in God. Quite honestly, I don't really know a formula to get here, but I just know that for Myra, there was no other option. I am desperate for Him and I rely upon his will in every situation. I know I am not the smartest person in the world, so I need Him. It just makes good common sense. I don't want to live a life of insanity; so trusting God and not me is the only way to go. The commonly coined definition of insanity is doing the same thing over and over again expecting different results. Neither the insane approach nor the crapshoot approach works for me. But knowing the will of God most certainly does!

    Don't be bamboozled. Live with purpose on purpose. God wants you to know His will. Ask Him what His will is in every situation. Wait for His guidance and then live in assurance that He is directing your path. It's that simple.

Scripture Meditations: Ephesians 5:17, Psalms 32:6-11, John 10:14, Psalms 118:8, Jeremiah 17:5-10

DAY 23: RESCUE 911

Insurance companies are the marketing champions of security for a monthly premium. They guarantee safety and help in hard times using catchy slogans to lure us in. "You're in good hands with Allstate."; "Get a piece of the rock."(Prudential) and "Get Met. It pays." are just a few insurance company slogans crafted to provide extra assurance that "in times of calamity, you are covered!" However, are their guarantees of help in crisis true? Have you ever needed a 911 rescue to get you out of the trouble you were in? Have you ever needed emergency assistance and actually got immediate assistance from an insurance company? Sometimes they take forever to pay a claim! What about the many companies who go out of business when too many large claims come in? Let's not even discuss the wait time on the automated service line that loops you into eternity rather than put your call in to an actual customer service representative. I often think they are hoping that they can wear you out with the waiting to avoid addressing the nature of your call.

AND, it's incredibly easy for them to drop you or increase your premium as a result of a claim—even though you've been paying premiums for the past 15 years. The one time you need them, you are penalized. It is all about the small print, fine lines and details that provide loopholes for the company, giving you less coverage than what you thought you were paying for. That's just a few of the "joys" and "uncertainties" of the insurance industry. I am so glad that my confidence is not in my insurance company in times of crisis.

Despite the many challenges of the insurance industry, there is still good news in these uncertain times! There is no state like being a citizen of the kingdom, and in the good hands of a loving Heavenly Father. He is the rock that provides all the assurance we need. Insurance policies are great wealth protection tools, but they are just far from infallibility. They lack the ability to provide you and your family total protection and complete coverage in every area of your lives! When you are a citizen of the kingdom of God, you have a foolproof insurance policy to cover you in times of crisis without fine print or hidden agendas.

One morning I awoke to a promise in scripture that says, "...before they call, I will answer and while they are yet speaking, I will hear." (Isaiah 5:24) The more I tried to lie in bed and just listen and meditate on that promise, the more I knew I had to get up and actually read it. So, I read it in several translations. I felt an intriguing invitation from the Holy Spirit and I knew that God was whispering a treasured secret to me in that moment. I didn't want to miss what He was saying. Here's what I read. This is going to bless you. Let's take a look at Isaiah 65:23:24 (KJV). "They shall not labour in vain, nor bring forth for trouble; for they are the seed of the blessed of the Lord, and their offspring with them. And it shall come to pass, that before they call, I will answer; and while they are yet speaking, I will hear."

While reading that scripture, I realized (my revelation from the Holy Spirit) that all of my work is not in vain. I did not birth my business/ministry so that it would bring me trouble. I am very blessed and my children are too; therefore, before I ever have to yell out for help, my loving and attentive Heavenly Father hears me and he has already answered. The New Living Translation says,

> They will not work in vain, and their children will not be doomed to misfortune. For they are people blessed by the, Lord and their children, too, will be blessed. I will answer them before they even call to me. While they are still talking to me about their needs, I will go ahead and answer their prayers!

God will not make me work without gain! Hallelujah, my labour is not in vain! My children's lives will be even better than my life and they will not be stuck in cycles of insanity, poverty or anything else that will limit their potential. They will enjoy God's riches and goodness. Both my seed and I are favoured by the Lord. His favour rains upon us and therefore, we are blessed. His favour goes before us in every situation. I do not have to worry about anything. I have an infallible insurance policy from the Lord that promises He is taking care of every one of my needs—even before I talk to him about what I think my needs are. When I begin to articulate my needs, He finishes my sentences. By the time I get to the end of my questions, He has already provided the answers.

The Good News Translation states it this way, "The work they do will be successful, and their children will not meet with disaster. I will bless them and their descendants for all time to come. Even before they finish praying to me, I will answer their prayers." Everything I touch will be successful. My children will not be met with disaster in life. It will be well with them. The Lord will bless not just my children, but also my children's children and my lineage forever more. We all have the promise of answered prayer. As long as we invite God into every situation, our prayers will be answered!

"They will never again work for nothing. They will never again give birth to children who die young. All my people will be blessed by the lord; I will provide for their needs before they ask, and I will help them while they are still asking for help." (New Century Version) Although in the past, I have worked and toiled with no recompense, that day is gone forever! My season has changed. I will be paid for my work. My children will live long lives and we will be blessed by the Lord. I have an eternal security and insurance policy that grants me provision for every one of my needs. I have to ask, because that's the law. But even when my strength is gone and my words are few, my loving father knows everything, including the sentiments of my heart that I will eventually articulate to him. Therefore, He springs into action and creates the provision even without hearing my voice!

That was worth getting out of bed! Thank you Holy Spirit for reminding me that day that the Lord is my Rescue 911 and the best insurance policy that I can ever own! Thank you Lord for being a loving Heavenly Father, who is comparable to nothing and no one!

Scripture Meditations: Isaiah 65:23-24, I John 5:14-15, Proverbs 13:22 & Proverbs 10:22

DO

DAY 24: FIRST THINGS FIRST

I don't know about you, but I have been guilty of putting the proverbial cart before the horse many times—especially when I am excited about a new task or a new season. I quickly find myself far up the road. Before too much damage is done or before I get too far ahead of the process, I am redirected. I turn around and go back to the starting point. You see, no matter how excited you are about seeing the end results of vision, there are some things that must be done first before you can get to the results!

Can you imagine an architect getting ahead of himself because he is excited about seeing the results of a building he has designed? What would happen if he went straight from the finished design on the drawing board to making the drawing a quick reality by bypassing all the necessary required steps? Imagine what would happen to his building (vision) if he refused to take the time to obtain the required permits and follow city ordinances. Imagine that he does not hire the qualified persons needed to make this drawing a safe and habitable reality. What if he chose people who were not necessarily qualified builders but he chose men who were just as excited as he was to see the quick results? Consider what the foundation of the structure would be like. Would there even be a foundation, because after all, you usually cannot see the foundation. Perhaps these unskilled builders would think that taking the time to build a proper foundation would only be a waste of their time because after all, they were in a hurry to see the building completed! An architect is a person *trained* to plan and design buildings, and to oversee their construction. We know in reality, it would never really happen this way. But have we ever been guilty of this imagined process in our daily lives? Have we ever tried to rush the process, bypass the necessary foundational steps to get to the manifestation of our vision or dreams? Well, before you go half-baked on this journey of envisioning, let us get a proper foundation! We must understand the principle of first things first!

St. Matthew 6:33 says, "But seek first his kingdom and his righteousness, and all these things will be given to you as well" (NIV). One of my most favorite Proverbs says, "Roll your works upon the Lord [commit and trust them wholly to Him; He will cause your thoughts to become agreeable to His will, and] so shall your plans be established *and* succeed.''" (Proverbs 16:3 Amp) These two passages give you dynamic tools for an amazing, worry free, successful life with proper foundation. I encourage you to meditate on these two passages over and over. Read them. Recite them. Learn them until they become as natural as breathing to you. They must become not just a part of you, but you! Let's consider their meanings.

"But seek ye first the kingdom and His righteousness." First means first. It means being before all others with respect to time, order, rank and importance. So, in order to maximize your purpose in life, you must FIRST seek the kingdom and His righteousness. What exactly does that mean? God's kingdom is His right way of doing things. It is his preeminent rule dictating your life. It means that you choose his ways, his ideas, his thoughts FIRST in every situation in your life. His opinions are not a second choice in your life. Before you even form an opinion or make a plan, ask Him first and then choose His choice.

I know that concept challenges you at your very core. I know for some, you were with me on every point that I shared right up until that last paragraph. Everything in you is now cringing. (I am actually feeling that even as I am writing, but, I am praying for you at this very moment!) I encourage you to stay with me. Keep reading. If you took a moment to meditate on what I said in the last paragraph, something deep inside of you recognizes this to be truth, but your mind just can't seem to grasp it. I know in order to embrace the concept of not doing things your way, but God's way takes a paradigm shift and an increased level of trust especially for most adults. We spent the bulk of our childhood lives anticipating the moment when we are officially grown and can make all of our own choices and decisions. The reality is, as we grow, we mature. If you grew up with good parents, you now realize that many of the rules we despised as children were put in place for our good, our learning and our protection. Some of the very restrictions that were placed on us, we now use in the rearing of our children because now we have a better understanding of why those rules are important. With God, it's even better than with good natural parents. Your natural parents with all of their love and goodness are still limited in their ability to know your purpose and consistently predict future outcomes. They are not infallible. This is not true with God. He is incapable of failing you.

    Think about it. God is omnipotent, omnipresent, and omniscient. He made you. He knows everything about you---including the intent of your heart. He knows everything about your past, present and future. He even knows that which is blind to you. He knows things you don't even know about yourself! With this vast insight and knowledge, why would it not be to my advantage to inquire of Him first? He knows all possible short cuts and outcomes. So, if you have matured to trust your good natural parents, how much more can your Heavenly Father be trusted? He knows what is best for you. His desire is never to take away your ability to be grown or to make choices. But His desire is to help you make choices that help you enjoy life and to assist you in maximizing your time and space in this world. He can be trusted. If He made you, then He wired you. He knows your tastes, likes and dislikes. You do not need to worry that He will give you something you can't handle or don't want. He wants the very best for His children and that is ALWAYS his motive! Our good natural parents had this same desire only they did not know everything that was really best for you. Some of their decisions were solely based on what they thought was best. Good and mature adults respect and appreciate their parents for doing what they thought was best. But only God really knows what is best. He is a very loving and caring Father.

    Now that we have discussed the first principle, now let's explore how Proverbs 16:3 comes into play. The steps are simple. "Roll YOUR works upon the Lord, commit and trust them wholly to Him. He will cause your thoughts to become agreeable to His will and so shall YOUR plans be established and succeed."

    I used to believe there was just no way that I could think like God or please Him entirely and be happy too. Then, I spiritually ingested this scripture and my entire thought process and belief system changed. I recognized that pleasing God was really a matter of the heart. If the focus of my desire changed from wanting to please me, to wanting God to be pleased, both of us would ultimately benefit. It is a matter of the heart. If I take what I have and give it to the Lord wholly; if I commit all my ways to Him, something supernatural occurs. This is the key, 'He will cause what I think to become agreeable to what He wants' and then what I do will bring me success and prosperity. Wow! That is simply amazing! It takes the pressure off of me. The struggle is taken out and the level of trust increases! God comes in and supernaturally changes everything!

So before you put the cart before the horse, get your foundation right. Before you use all of your energy to bring to pass pointless and futile endeavours, do first things first and watch how effective you become and with great ease!

Scripture Meditations: Matthew 6:33, Proverbs 16:3 Amplified, Psalms 37:4

DAY 25: THE REVELATION OF KENNY ROGERS

On November 15, 1978, American country music artist Kenny Rogers released the recorded song written by Don Schlitz that would later cause him in 1980 to receive the Grammy award for best male country vocal performance. The song, The Gambler has been making history ever since.

Many years later while sitting in my car, I heard the song, The Gambler, come on the radio of the car sitting next to me. It caught my attention and, believe it or not, the Holy Spirit instantly arrested me. I knew God was speaking to me. Of course, the whole song did not apply, but certain words and phrases were direct words from God to me at that time! The words are, *"You got to know when to hold 'em, know when to fold 'em, know when to walk away and know when to run."*

You see, at that time I was working for a ministry that I loved, but it was time to go. I was wrestling in my spirit, but in the natural, I was very comfortable. I lived well and had a guaranteed paycheck that was not too bad. I liked the house I lived in and the car that I drove and had actually grown to love the people. Why should I upset the applecart? Life was good. That is the page I was on despite how many times God nudged me about leaving. It was only three years before that God clearly opened the door for me to work in this place, but now that same Lord was troubling my spirit about it being time to go. It might have been easier to make a decision to leave if I had the guarantee of another position that afforded me all the comforts of this one. I had no other job offer and no certainty other than the Word of the Lord to me and the 'knowing in my knower!'

I thought about it. I had been in this place before—the place where I had to choose to obey God or to obey myself. After The Gambler went off the radio, the Holy Spirit began to remind me of the story of Abram, before he became Abraham in Genesis 12.

Now the LORD had said to Abram: Get out of your country, from your family and from your father's house, To a land that I will show you. I will make you a great nation; I will bless you and make your name great; and you shall be a blessing. I will bless those who bless you, and I will curse him who curses you; And in you all the families of the earth shall be blessed." So Abram departed as the LORD had spoken to him.

From that passage, I remembered a principle about the benefits of obeying God. There is a price to pay to obey God, but I am a witness that the price is never greater than the reward! His requests are always for a purpose and backed by His rewards. In essence, God is faithful and He always makes it up to you.

I encourage you today to be different from most people. Learn from The Gambler and know when it is time to walk away and when it is time to run. Too many people stay stuck in situations, circumstances, relationships, jobs, cities and even churches because they are afraid to leave what they know---their comfort zones. They do not want to take risks. May I suggest to you that if you have a "knowing" in your spirit that it is time to make a change, DO IT AFRAID! Be obedient to God and take the leap! Sometimes your only mode of transportation out of a situation is a leap of faith! God will catch you lead you, guide you and provide for you. Be sensitive to know not only what God said, but hear what He is presently saying. Be so sensitive to Him that you are open to hear His heart about new direction and instruction for your life.

Scripture Meditations: Hebrews 11, Genesis 12, Psalms 32:8, Deuteronomy 8:18

DAY 26: RISKY BUSINESS

Although I am not a big movie buff, some years ago I had the pleasure of watching Spider-Man III and can I say, wow! It was a very deep movie. I could not stop thinking about it. The next week I taught a Bible Study Lesson on it because the movie moved me so much. Yes, I taught a bible study lesson inspired by Spider Man III. The movie was so filled with revelation. If you have not seen Spider-Man III, I will try to make my point without giving away the entire storyline. The storyline features Spider-Man, our resident spider hero displaying a surprising dark side. The "dark side" personality of Spider-Man changed everything about him-his psyche, his actions, his disposition, his thinking and even his normal red and blue Spider Man outfit changed into an all black one. (Now you can see why I called it his dark side.) How could this happen to our friendly neighborhood hero? How did this character change from being a wonderful and innocent boyish crusader for justice to an evil villain covered with what I have come to label as the "blob?" He allowed the seed of unforgiveness to germinate in his heart. I entitled the bible study lesson, "The Devastating Effects of Unforgiveness". (You can order it from our online bookstore). Unforgiveness brings total destruction and devastation on so many levels. Understand my friend; refusing to forgive someone who has hurt or wronged you is risky business.

There was a scene in the movie where the "blob" initially shows up as a very small thing in the beginning. The "blob" was a black gooey liquid that looked like tar. It was lurking around in Spider-Man's house, especially near his bed. You only saw the "blob" surface when Spider-Man began to meditate on his feelings of anger and hurt about a situation in the past that he could not change. The more he thought about the past situation, the angrier he became. Resentment grew and the desire for vengeance became his focus. As he fell deeper and deeper into unforgiveness, the blob got bigger and until eventually, it got on him, became one with him and totally took over his personality. The blob literally turned him into a complete and totally different man. Unforgiveness has the capacity to change who you are. It becomes bigger than you!

Opportunities for anger, resentment and unforgiveness are always near and awaiting the right moment to move from the outside to the inside of our hearts. What is on the inside of you will eventually be clearly displayed on the outside. The opportunity to become hurt, angry or harbor resentment will always be present. The marriage of unforgiveness and evil action takes place in our hearts and the result is clearly seen through our dispositions and attitudes. The blob can overtake us the moment we refuse to release and forgive the offenses. It happens when we decide to become a crusader for vengeance, executing our own justice. It occurs when we think or say things like, "They are going to pay for what they did to me." or "I'm going to get them back!" It also occurs when we simply choose to "write them off" or act as if they don't exist! You may think that just because you have removed yourself from the circle of friends or foes; or choose not to deal with individuals who have hurt, wronged or disappointed you, that it is well with you. But if there is just a smidgen of anger or resentment in your heart towards those persons, there is a great chance that you are holding unforgiveness in your heart. Unfortunately, the old adage, "out of sight – out of mind" does not apply here. Unforgiveness, my friend, is risky business and enough of it will make you act out of character and in ways that are out of control.

Unforgiveness, like most things, begins as a seed. It begins as a small thing, but the potential of a seed is not just a tree. The potential of a seed is an entire forest. Every seed goes through a germination process. To germinate means to cause to sprout or develop; to come into being; to evolve; to begin to grow. When you foster an environment for unforgiveness in your heart, unforgiveness will grow. It will evolve and develop more and more. Before you know it, it's a huge garden, and then it becomes an entire forest too big to manage. Unforgiveness impairs your vision, skews your judgment, makes you bitter, uncontrollable and has the potential to turn you into someone that even you don't recognize.

Unforgiveness short-circuits your life. It imprisons you. It becomes a wedge between you and a fulfilled, successful future. It takes energy and happiness from you and robs you of peace and victory. Unforgiveness works hard against you, but empowers those who you choose not to forgive. It actually gives that individual power over you. It allows them to control you much like a remote control has power over a television. Unforgiveness allows the other person to push your buttons and make you act in ways you never imagined. Now think about it. Do you really want to empower the individual who has wronged you by giving them that much power over you? If you have ever been imprisoned to unforgiveness then you clearly understand how everything changes when the person that offended you comes around—your mood, feelings, actions and entire disposition changes in their presence.

I remember how this type of imprisonment feels. Many years ago, I experienced a relationship that went really sour before it ever got started. This individual was not only older but she was in authority over me, both at church and work. So many awful things happened during the course of this relationship and at first, I was not the person with the problem. I was able to ignore her issues with me. Eventually, I could no longer ignore them and I began to address every offense. Every evil thing she did became personal to me. I felt like since no one would defend me, I had to defend myself. Others saw the mistreatment and even received poor treatment from her themselves. This justified my anger and defensiveness; and added fuel to the fire of my resentment. I hated her. Prior to this season, worship was so easy for me. It was easy to get into the presence of the Lord, but in this season the moment she walked in church, I got angry, cold, bitter and dry. I would literally stop trying to make a connection with God, sit down and give in to the anger. This was so out of character for me. The sad part is that I lived like this for several years. I became so bitter that I couldn't even cry. It was so awful. I remember counseling sessions with my Pastor regarding the issue. He asked me, "What happened to the sweet and sensitive Myra I knew?" I responded, "She happened! And I'm sick of it and I hate her!" My Pastor said, "That's impossible, because the Bible says, 'the love of God is shed abroad in your heart by the Holy Ghost!" He said, "So if you are saved, there's no way you can hate anybody from your heart, for real." Can you imagine what I said? The "blob" had completely overtaken me by this time because my response was, "Well, I guess I'm not saved!" Really??? How did I become convinced of such a ridiculous lie? I allowed unforgiveness to germinate in my heart!

The opposite of unforgiveness is forgiveness. The power of forgiveness works in your favor. It empowers you. It is liberating freedom and refreshing to those who forgive. Forgiveness brings healing and release from past hurts and disappointments. Forgiving others is difficult at times, but it frees you from prison. It releases you to be controlled only by you. It allows your creative energy to flow and opens the heavens up for you. Forgiveness allows the favor of the Lord to reign in your life. Mark 11:24-26 [Amplified] says,

For this reason I am telling you, whatever you ask for in prayer, believe (trust and be confident) that it is granted to you, and you will [get it]. And whenever you stand praying, if you have anything against anyone, forgive him *and* let it drop (leave it, let it go), in order that your Father Who is in heaven may also forgive you your [own] failings *and* shortcomings *and* let them drop. *But if you do not forgive, neither will your Father in heaven forgive your failings and shortcomings.*

We can choose to remain hurt, angry or resentful about offenses when they arise or we can use the power of forgiveness to release the offense. Unforgiveness is not worth the risk of losing your peace, victory, and the favor of God! Ask the Holy Spirit to help you forgive. He will empower you and He will strengthen you to do it. To live any other way is risky business!

Scripture Meditations: Mark 11:24-26, Matthew 5:44, Luke 11:4

DAY 27: A LESSON ON BALANCE

Some years ago I was given the opportunity to choose a topic to speak on at a conference hosted in Atlanta. One of the topics that really resonated in my spirit was 'Who is ministering to you while you are ministering to them?' The topic resounded so loud within me because I remembered when God began to teach me balance. You would think that through the various schoolings, tests and corrections I have encountered, I would have the concept of balance down packed by now. What's most amazing is that every time I feel as though I have 'arrived in this area'—that I have learned my lesson and now "own" the proverbial T-Shirt—life presents yet another challenge that causes me to refocus and realign...AGAIN.

How thankful I am, for the ability to jump right back on the Potter's wheel so that I can just "get it" and move on to the next challenge that life brings. Certainly, life is kinetic—-always moving, always offering "new"—new challenges, new situations, new obstacles, new encounters, new relationships, new assignments, new tasks, and new opportunities for growth, death, burials, resurrections, tears and the like. Such is life!

My primary motivational gift is administration. God gifts administrators to multi-task and organize. We often carry the load for visionaries. We work on many tasks at once, so it is very easy for administrators to lose a sense of balance. What I have found is that in order for Myra to keep this "balance thing" in check, the Holy Spirit must constantly be at work in me. Trust me, He means for me to stay balanced! He is committed to helping me with that.

Let us consider that question, 'Who is ministering to you while you are ministering to them?' I know that the word "ministering" is often reserved for most as a churchy word for what preachers do. So, perhaps you are not a public speaker, does that mean that you do not minister. Not so! Believe it or not, you too are in ministry! Let me prove it to you. According to the dictionary, to minister means to give aid or service. Enough said! Whether you are a mom or dad, a pastor or a teacher, a business owner or an employee or just a person who is alive, chances are at some point you minister (giving aid or service) to someone!

I am a woman, nurturer, author, wife, Co-Pastor, mother, auntie, stepmom, daughter, sister, business owner, mentor, life coach, preacher, teacher, transformational speaker, confidant, bookkeeper, administrator, short order cook, janitor, event planner, travel agent, chauffeur, counselor and friend. I sometimes find myself overwhelmed, feeling exhausted, misunderstood, unappreciated, unaccomplished, unfulfilled and on a "banana peel with NOTHING ELSE left to give." That is usually when someone comes along asking for ONE MORE THING!!!!! Maybe, that is just my life. Perhaps I am the only one guilty of ALLOWING myself to get to this place. Yep, I often say, "This doesn't feel like cinnamon and spice and everything nice. Isn't that for what girls are made of?" Every time I find myself "here," there are two things I recall to my mind so I can have hope. **First, balance is the key to a successful life. Second, I was NOT created to be a SUPERHERO!**

If you are a man reading today's meditation, I can only write this part from my perspective as a woman. As you read it, male or female, I think you will have an appreciation of what we are all called to do. You may also be able to fill in the blanks of the parts that are not written here from the male's perspective for all that men do. We are all contributors and we all have our God-given assignments. I have great appreciation for how God wired men and women. It is the Lord's doing. My spiritual mom, Debra Gibson, often shares that "generally speaking, God has wired men to be mono and women to be stereo." What does this mean? This suggests that women can do several things at once, while men often work well one task at a time. Again, this is neither bad nor good. It just speaks to our differences. That is just the way God wired the sexes.

This is often the way it goes for me. WONDER WOMAN POWERS, ACTIVATE! Simply stated, perfectly said. We are indeed "IT." We have the wiring of a regular multi-tasking superhero. Think about it. Who else gets up in the morning, HAPPY— making sure breakfast is prepared or at least available. Then get dressed and ready for another day, and not just yourself but the kids also. They have to be out on time, school papers signed and checked and in their book bags. Who else cooks dinner while talking on the phone, counseling or consoling a friend, does the laundry and housework while helping the kids with their homework? Then if that is not enough, before the evening is over we have done it all. We have made grocery lists and to-do-lists for the rest of the week; scheduled all the kid's appointments; played games and spent quality time with the kids. We have ironed and prepared everyone's clothing for the next day, combed hair, packed lunches and checked homework. We have spent 2.2 seconds figuring out what we are going to wear the next day, kissed boo-boo's, put out fires, greeted Hubby with a big kiss and a warm reception. We have listened to his day (concerns or challenges), given him solutions (although you made sure he thought it was his idea), made HIM feel like the KING of the castle and then ministered on every level to HIS needs. Of course, this all comes after ministering to ALL the other needs of the house, the kids, work, and yes, even the family's pets. The insane thing is that somehow we are able to lay down, rest and start another day the same way, at the same pace. Then we wonder why THEY think we can do it all? Lord knows we try to do it all. I find that most women really do buy into the invisible superwoman sign that they wear under their clothes. They really think, 'If I don't do it, it won't get done! And if it doesn't get done...?"

Today's lesson is all about balance— male or female, homemaker or business entrepreneur. If you are living in a cycle of busyness and ineffectiveness, STOP IT! Take Back Your Power! The Holy Spirit has taught me to take my power back by prioritizing. Perhaps you should ask yourself some of these questions:

- Does ALL of this have to be done today? Or this week? Or this month?

- Is this task(s) consistent with the mission and purpose statement for my life?

- Am I using my time and resources effectively? Am I the one that should do this?

- Am I using my words effectively or efficiently?

- Is this my good idea or is this God's idea?

- MOST IMPORTANTLY, Have I requested the Holy Spirit's Help today?

You see, God's plan for us is to be fruitful and multiply, not busy and ineffective. Our success depends upon us doing what we are supposed to be doing in the timing that we are supposed to do it. At some point, we have to re-evaluate what we do, shut some things down, reassess needs, delegate, bury some stuff and create systems that afford us the opportunity to maximize our space and place.

We must do first things first. We must first minister to the Holy Spirit daily because He is waiting to minister to you. Daily He provides strength, direction and wisdom.
We must be deliberate about ministering to OURSELVES. For some of us that requires a paradigm shift because it sounds selfish. The reality is, after God, YOU are your greatest priority! To help you with balance ask yourself, "How have I ministered to the Lord and myself today?

Scripture Meditations: Proverbs 11:1 AMP, Nehemiah 4:15, Galatians 2:21

DAY 28: STAY THE COURSE

God is always communicating with us through diverse and various ways. Some say, "I never hear God speak." Trust me, He is speaking, but to hear Him, we must tune into the right frequency. I have noticed that God often speaks about things that may seem irrelevant to our lives at the time. We get sweet reminders from the Holy Spirit about something He promised or we hear him speak words of peace to our spirits in times of turmoil. Many times, it seems that He doesn't speak during times of difficulty when we really need to hear Him.

God knows how to communicate with you so that you understand what He is saying. You know that some of the things that come to your mind are not because you are so smart, especially when the thought just comes out of nowhere! Often, the incredible ideas that you "thought of" is information your human spirit received from the Holy Spirit who is now giving illumination to your mind. It is just that simple; and you only gave credit to your thoughts.

Man is a spirit, He possesses a soul and He lives on the inside of a body. There are three parts to you: spirit, soul and body. God communicates Spirit to spirit. He does not communicate with your mind. He speaks to your spirit. God communicates with us in all sorts of ways: through scripture, through things that we see and even through our experiences. Sometimes He speaks to our spirits through the words of a song, a poem or even a conversation with a child. I have learned the importance of writing down what He says and finding ways to hold on to it, because He does not waste His words. He may not repeat Himself. Sometimes we think little of what He says because we do not understand the purpose of what He is saying in the moment.

Here is an example. While riding in a car on my way to Knoxville, TN, looking at the beautiful mountains daydreaming and thinking about how great, majestic God is, out of nowhere, these words came to mind: "Stay the course!" Because I have experienced this many times before, I knew that God was communicating something He wanted me to know. It felt so refreshing and assuring. I wrote it down, dated it and pondered it. I knew it was good advice. I knew it was a good word. It felt good to me to hear it at the time, even though I was not thinking about it. To my knowledge, I have never actually said that sentence before. To my knowledge, I have never given anyone that advice or instruction. But, God told me again, "Just stay the course!"

    Little did I know, how much in days to come, I would draw constant strength, direction, hope and peace from that simple phrase! You see at the time God spoke those words to me, things in my life were okay. Nothing was wrong. Then, out of nowhere, everything was wrong. I entered into one of the most difficult seasons of my life and ministry. Everything seemed hard: marriage, people, finances and ministry all at once. More times than not, I have wanted to leave, quit, run away and start a whole new life doing all new things with all new people. Now, I am sure you may not be able to identify with that place and that is okay because each of our journeys are different, therefore our God-given grace for situations are different. I actually had to fight myself (my will, my mind, my emotions) and convince myself to be still; make no sudden moves or drastic changes. I had to force myself to think (meditate) on the word of the Lord that was spoken to me in that car that day. "Just stay the course!" God meant for me to just keep doing what He told me to do and nothing new despite the turbulence.

    A few months prior to that, the Holy Spirit said to me "Do it according to what I have shown you in the mount." In the mount represented when I was up with Him in prayer (breathing), and He communicated direction to me. What that meant was to go back to the things that He originally told me and showed me at the beginning before the turbulence and the difficulty. He gave me instructions to review His plans, will and vision for my life and ministry. I know that "according to the pattern that I showed you in the mount" is biblical jargon, but the two words together provided a staying power that kept me sane when everything and almost everyone seemed crazy. I realized that I had exactly what I needed to carry me through this very difficult season of my life.

For years, I have encouraged the discipline of journaling. Many people have said to me, "I am just not a writer. I just do not like to journal. I don't like to write." Might I suggest that you adopt journaling as a lifestyle? When I say journaling, consider what I really mean. I am not suggesting that you write down what you do each day. I am suggesting that you have a place –a book where you write down your thoughts and questions to God, and more importantly, His thoughts to you! Date them. Trust me, when He speaks its precious and He is not obligated to speak again. If you write down the things He communicates to you in your seasons of comfort, joy and bliss, you will be able to go back and recall to your mind exactly what you need when the days are cloudy and your vision is obscure. There will be times when you cannot feel Him, hear Him or even trace Him. In those moments, you need a personal word from the Lord to remind you to hold steady—to make no sudden changes, to do it as he showed you in the mount, and stay the course so that you might look up and live!

Scripture Meditations: Exodus 25:40 & I Corinthians 15:57-58

DAY 29: LET THE UMPIRE DO HIS JOB

Do you ever feel like your mind is filled with clutter and that you have so many things to do and so many decisions to make; yet, you do not have the first clue about where to start? Do you ever feel like you do not have the energy or the knowledge of where to go to get the right answers? I know that place. I have been so overwhelmed in my life and I have felt great pressure; the kind of pressure that makes me feel like so many people are counting on me and there are so many things at stake. My decisions HAVE to be right—perfect!

When I give into that pressure, I find that my life is crazy! I don't sleep and do not have the ability to focus, not to mention how difficult I become, until I shake myself and remember what I know! What I know in those times is that this place of "crazy" is whack! God is not the author of confusion, but of peace!

The Apostle Paul said, "Let the peace (soul harmony which comes) from Christ rule (act as an umpire continually) in your hearts [deciding and settling with finality all questions that arise in your minds]." Colossians 3:15 (AMP). Even if you are not a big fan and have little knowledge of baseball, like me, most of us can imagine a baseball game between two very competitive teams without an umpire. You guessed it! The game would end quickly, but not before utter chaos takes over!

God wired you with a 'hidden man of the heart.' It is your spirit being that you cannot see, but he is there. If you are born again, he (your hidden man) gets his information from the Holy Spirit. That means he connects to a different channel from the chaos that we sometimes experience in life. He lives by and tunes into a different frequency. It is the frequency of Heaven. His job and His desire is to lead and guide you into all truth. Did you hear me? HIS job is to lead you and guide you into all truth! He is the umpire of your soul. It is HIS job to help you play the game of life in peace and harmony.

The primary way he does his job is by allowing you to experience a peace on the inside even when everything on the outside is CRAZY!

Think about it. Haven't you ever experienced this? Perhaps you got some news or something very awful happened to you. You may have been hurt or stung by the problem, but way down deep inside there was a "weird" feeling that did not line up with what was going on in your head or your reality. During those times, I would try to work up a state of panic, a tear or some "feeling" of fear or anxiety. I would even ask myself, "Is something wrong with me? Shouldn't I be worried or really concerned about this?" In those moments of questioning myself, I was experiencing the umpire of peace! In baseball, the umpire is the person who officiates the game; enforces the rules, makes judgment calls on plays and handles the disciplinary actions. The umpire of peace in your life officiates the game. He is enforcing God's rules & making judgment calls on what is right & wrong for you. He is the voice of your conscience that disciplines you for bad choices & gives you a feeling of great accomplishment when you make good choices. He brings comfort in the middle of life's chaos and assures you that God has you.

So, the next time you get to a place where you are overwhelmed with life's situations, stop trying to be the umpire. Your job is to show up, dressed in proper attire and ready to follow the rules of the game. The umpire's job is to make the calls. He knows how and sees what you cannot see. He is the final authority in the game. So, slow down. Cooperate with him and then just go the way of peace. You do not have to understand it, and chances are you will not. This peace is way down deep inside of you. It is not a head thing; it is a heart thing. Sometimes doing nothing is the best thing to do. "Peace I leave with you; My peace I give to you; not as the world gives do I give to you. Do not let your heart be troubled, nor let it be fearful." John 14:27 (NAS) Make it a great day!

Scripture Meditations: John 14:27, Colossians 3:15

DAY 30: SMOKE SCREENS & REAL FIRE

I am reminded of how many times I gave the enemy more credit than God. I didn't realize how, so it was definitely unintentional. I often mediated and taught others how the enemy is always putting up 'smoke screens' designed to hinder us, make us afraid, discourage and block us from aggressively progressing in life. When we are facing the enemy's smoke screens, we seldom realize until later that it was just a smoke screen! In the moment, we tend to view the barriers, difficulties and challenges as real fire therefore, we refuse to move forward because we are either zapped of our strength to fight due to smoke inhalation or we fear the effects of fire. We submit to the apparent reality that we are no match for it! Unfortunately, it is only in retrospect that we realize it was just a bluff—a puff of smoke but no real fire. What a waste! That is exactly what happens when we live by our natural senses.

I looked at two distinct definitions found in the Merriam-Webster Dictionary for the term smoke screen. I saw something amazing and quite liberating! One definition defined a smoke screen as "something designed to obscure, confuse, or mislead." We usually view smoke screens from the perspective of our enemy. This gives the negativity in our lives the upper hand. If this perspective is accurate, then the believer is always at a disadvantage because we are always caught by surprise and never know when we are facing a smoke screen or real fire. We then spend too much assessing the situation.

The second definition is what changed my perspective and has me jumping in my boots! The second definition says, "A smoke screen is a screen of smoke to hinder enemy observation of a military force, area, or activity." The Holy Spirit reminded me that my loving Heavenly Father always has the upper hand and He too produces smoke screens, not against me, but for me! Look at the definition again, this time with my emphasis. "A screen of smoke to *hinder enemy observation* of a military force *(me)*, area *(my personal stuff i.e. my children, home, possessions etc.), or activities (the things that I am doing in life especially for the Kingdom)!* I am in the army of God and I am a force to be reckoned with! God does not allow the enemy to know everything about me and His direction for my life. God hinders the enemy's ability to observe some things about me. God covers me! He alone is responsible for my care, provision and protection! Doesn't that make you want to jump in your boots too! The enemy is confused and misled by God. His eyes burn and he's really the one who suffers smoke inhalation due to the smoke screens my Heavenly Father erects for me! God does not play fair! He holds true to His nature. He is an all-consuming fire! He is the God who answers by fire! So, the enemy is not just looking at a smoke screen, he is confronted by the fire of God. There is a real wall of fire around me! That is why no weapon formed against me will prosper!

My husband preached a sermon in which he said, **"Praise God that you were able to even get to the fire!"** Now, at first that was not so thrilling to me, although I went through the motions in church and I sent up "a praise" as instructed! I began to say in my mind, "I don't want to praise God for that! I don't want to be in the fire anymore! I'm tired of fire!" As he continued his sermon, a real praise was ignited within me! He said, "Some people didn't even make it to the fire. They died. They were consumed. Although this fire that you're now in is heated seven times hotter than it has ever been before, it HAS NOT CONSUMED YOU! It consumed others, but not you!" Then the Pastor really provoked my praise! He said, "…and although you went into this fire BOUND….you are walking around in it with the fourth man (God), LOOSED and unharmed!" Wow! Think about it. You may go through some real fire: challenges and difficult life situations, but you are still alive. If the situations could take you out, you would have already been taken out! It's just that simple. God is with you. Your life is hid with Christ in God, so you are protected and covered. Go ahead; don't be afraid. Walk around in the fire. God is with you!

Am I inspiring you to breathe today? I am challenging you to change your perspective of the "fire" in your life right now! Live by the gift of your sixth sense, your faith in God. Recognize that in the past, the enemy of our soul never had to engage in real war against us to defeat us because we defeated ourselves. We fell into the trap of His distractions, which often came as smoke screens and fiery trials. Know that when we become so distracted with the challenges in our lives, we lose our focus. That's where he gains ground. When we lose our focus, we miss the mark (our goals) because we are paying too much attention to the wrong things. Regain your focus! Fulfilling your purpose in life is the most important thing. Our God is more powerful than anything that comes our way and nothing catches Him by surprise. He's got you covered from the enemy! Go forth today with the right focus and the right perspective! Get up and go get 'er done! Have a great and victorious day!

Scripture Meditations: Deuteronomy 4:24; 1 Kings 18:24; Isaiah 54:17; Daniel 3

DAY 31: PRAYER STILL WORKS!

I sang a song in church as a child that says, "I know prayer changes things. I know prayer changes things. Men ought to always pray and never faint. I know prayer changes things." There have never been truer words spoken! What I have learned however, is that sometimes it is not the "things" that are always changed by prayer. I learned that prayer changes me! Whether prayer changes "things" or "me", I appreciate the results of prayer.

Throughout scripture, God shows us how He waits for us to invite Him into our situations. He comes to rescue, deliver, give direction and grant what is needed. Have you ever prayed thinking you knew exactly what needed to be done and when it was all said and done, the answer was granted but not the answer you thought you needed? Have you ever panicked about a situation and as time went on your perspective changed but the situation did not? That is God changing you. Remember He is your loving Father. He knows everything you need and always has your best interest at heart. Never stop praying because prayer always works!

Prayer is simply communication with God. Notice I said communication "with God" and not only "to God." Often when we pray we go through our list of requests and concerns and then end with 'Amen' and hurry on our way. Communication, however, is a two-way process. Not only should we talk to God, but we should wait and allow Him to communicate with us. When we finish our discourse, we should spend time sitting quietly in His presence. This allows us to focus. This allows Him to infuse us with strength, direction and everything we need for the day. Trust me , it happens even when you can't feel it. Allowing God to breathe into us and our situations changes us because the power of prayer still works!

Prayer is a powerful connection between man and His God. Prayer is one of the greatest reservoirs given to the believer, yet it is one of the least tapped resources given to the body of Christ. Prayer is the one vehicle that can ascend man from earth to the throne room of God. It is the one thing that can release angels and all of the powers of heaven on a believer's behalf in less than a nanosecond. When I say prayer works, I am not talking about the "Our Father's Prayer," or "Now I lay me down to sleep" prayer. I'm not even talking about that nervous, begging thing people do when they are in a state of panic or desperation. I'm not talking about all those holy phrases and the King James Version people often use trying to communicate aloud with God. "O thou greatest God of the universe, thou knowest all things…" I'm not talking about the kind of "prayer" that is a person's last resort, "Well we've tried everything else, now let us pray." Prayer must be your first resort. When man has reached his end and has done all that he can do, REALLY, God's just getting his boots on!

If you have enlisted in God's army then you are commanded to be a good soldier. He gave you weapons to fight this war of life. Your weapons are mighty weapons: the blood of Jesus, the Word of God, the power of the Holy Spirit and yes, the power of prayer! These are your weapons of mass destruction! The enemy of your soul knows how precious to God and how powerful a believer's prayer life can be. That's why he makes sure you don't have one. He enjoys assisting you in being lazy. He loves bringing questions to your mind about the effectiveness of prayer. "Is this really working?" "Is there really anything to this?" "If God's going to do what he wants to do anyway, why bother praying? He does all of this to bring doubt and render you ineffective in prayer.

Whatever you are facing in your life right now, know that your communication with God makes all the difference in the world. Don't let the deceiver deceive you. Open your mouth and pray to your Heavenly Father. Invite Him into the situation, because the power of prayer still works!

Thirteen Secrets for a Successful Prayer Life

1. Remain in right-relationship with the Father. Psalm 91:1

2. Treat others right. Mark 11:24-26 & I Peter 3:7

3. Pray to the Father In the Name of Jesus. John 16:23-24

4. Trust that the Holy Spirit helps you pray even when you don't know what to say or how to pray. Romans 8:26

5. Mediate on and recognize your frailty and His greatness, your inability and His Great ability. Ephesians 3:20

6. Ascertain the will of God. I John 5:14-15

7. Don't ask amiss. James 4:38

8. Believe that you received WHEN YOU PRAY, then know it's done. Mark 11:24

9. Boost your prayer life by using the Power of Agreement. Matthew 18:19-20

10. Pray in the Spirit then, fight the GOOD fight of faith. Jude 1:20

11. It doesn't matter what it looks like--fight! I Timothy 6:12

12. Release your angels. Hebrews 1:14

13. Trust the Father's love and care for you. I Peter 5:7 & Psalms 55:22

Scripture Meditations: **Mark 14:38**, I Thess. 5:17, Philippians 4:6

DAY 32: BETTER NOT BITTER

Bad things happen to good people all the time. Sometimes the negative things we experience in life are attributed to a combination of generational issues, ignorance or poor choices. Other problems arise for which there seems to be no cause, reason or explanation. There are times when we feel as though we did our due diligence prior to encountering the problem or situation, but the outcome was still a disaster. Much of what happens in life just doesn't seem fair. There are things we experience that are so horrible that it is hard to wrap our minds around what really happened and why. We try to make sense of the incident so that we can move on, but the more we try to retrace our steps in hopes of understanding what went wrong, the less we understand. Some of these experiences really rock our worlds and challenge us to the core. When our perception of our negative experiences is wrong, those experiences can change us in ways that are not beneficial. We can become skeptical, cynical and even bitter. I challenge you to allow negative situations to make you "better" and not bitter! After all, it is your choice.

Life has "schools." I define "life's schools" as a plethora of seasons, situations, relationships, or experiences designed to make you better, although in the process it seems you're worse off than before. The interesting thing about "life's schools" is that you don't get the opportunity to choose your courses. You don't pick the times or the days of your classes. And you are not allowed to choose your teachers or classmates. No. Life does that for you. Some "courses" are harder than others. Some "courses" hurt more than others. In some "courses", you lose more than in others. The schools of life will ultimately create new visions, new dreams, new systems, new methods and new means to sustain a new way of living. It catapults you to unprecedented greatness when you allow it. One of the greatest things about the school of life is that it develops greater wisdom for those who pay attention and pass the tests. "Wisdom is the principle thing…" (Proverbs 4:7) Wisdom is far greater than knowledge. Wisdom is your ability to use the knowledge you have gained appropriately. You can gain a lot of knowledge from reading books, but if you don't know how and when to apply the knowledge to your current situation, then that knowledge lacks power. We must embrace the lessons that life teaches, actively engage in its classes and pass every test.

Although you are not allowed to choose the courses, you will always get to choose how you use the materials provided. I have learned that in order to graduate to the next level in life you must pass the test or you will have to take the test again. That is the reason why many people go through the same types of things over and over again. They have not learned their lesson, and therefore they cannot graduate to the next level in life. In life, there will always be tests, but taking the same test over and over again simply means, clearly you've not grasped the course objectives. You simply have not learned the point. You have not figured out the main idea.

In recent days, my husband and I involuntarily enrolled in a course from the business school of life that, if experienced a few years ago, would have rocked our world. This encounter had the potential to wreak havoc in the financial state of our family, impact our integrity and destroy us. It was a classic case of a business partnership gone wrong. Well, a bit more than a classic case, this partnership experience was really, really bad! The scenario included all the gut-wrenching factors of deceit, betrayal, and embezzlement. It happened to us by people that we thought we knew—people we trusted for over five years and assumed to be outstanding Christians and friends. We learned of some of the infractions nearly a year before the partnership came to an end. We experienced something similar before, but nothing to the degree we were dealing with in this situation.

We are grateful for all the lessons learned from our past experiences. Because of them, we knew how to wait on the wisdom of God and be sensitive to His voice for direction in this situation. Without that wisdom, we would have not been able to be still, wait and hear. I believe that the highest order of discipline is learning to wait on God. I cannot lie to you, in the beginning; I wanted to respond in my flesh with a knockout, drag-out fight! But maturity set in and we waited to allow wisdom to set things in motion. In life, unfortunately, you don't get an instruction manual that tells you how to deal with every situation that arises. Sometimes there is no quick fix or fast remedy. There are times when you just have to wait.

     Timing is of the essence. Waiting for God's instruction helps you not to act prematurely and create an even greater mess. Waiting paves the way for wisdom. It really seemed as though we were the ones loosing. It seemed as though the ungodly was prospering. But, I know how spiritual principles work. It's just a matter of time before the principle of sowing and reaping takes effect. After my personal fits of anger and turmoil subsided, my instructions from God became clear: "Keep your heart and motives pure; stay focused on your assignment!" I received an amazing immediate peace. The wisdom that was imparted to me for the situation was priceless. A week before the partnership came to an end I was in the car driving waiting for the light to change when I noticed the clouds. They were white and bright and filled with movement. I sensed God was communicating to my spirit, "You passed the test!" What a wonderful feeling of relief. At that moment, I had a renewed indescribable excitement about our future.

     Now I can clearly see how this experience aligns with my personal mission statement. A part of my mission in life is to live my life to be a blessing to the lives of men. I can't wait to share with others the wisdom gained through this experience. It is certainly fuel for the journey ahead! Most people share information or knowledge based upon what they learned from books or others. But it's more impactful when someone's life experience qualifies them to impart wisdom. You know the difference! That's me! I decided to allow this betrayal to make me better and not bitter. I have increased in wisdom and I am prepared for my next level.   Next, maybe I'll write Breathe for Business. I'm sure it will bless your life! The next time you get the opportunity to take a course in one of life's schools, understand the lessons, pass all of your tests and let them make you better and not bitter!

Scripture Meditations: Proverbs 4, Psalm 37, Psalm 73, Galatians 6:7

DAY 33: I CANNOT AFFORD TO BE USELESS IN THIS SEASON

I love a good parable. There is such wisdom to be extracted and gained. There is a parable in Matthew 25 about three servants. Take the time to read the parable. I think you will be able to appreciate it.

Here are some of my observations from the parable as found in St. Matthew 25:14-30 and the practical application of the lessons gained from this parable:

1. *The Master gave everyone talents/gifts according to their individual ability.*
   The Creator God of this universe knows how he made you and how he wired you. He knows the gifts He gave you and the extent of your capacity—(your abilities) to multiply and reproduce those gifts. Each servant was given something, but their capacities differed.

2. *The gifts given did not belong to the servants. The gifts actually belonged to the Master.*
   The servants merely had stewardship of the gift(s). The gifts entrusted were the property of the Master! We have all been entrusted with gift(s) that we did not have to work for to receive. However, these gifts require that we manage and put each gift to use. The gift(s) really do not belong to you, but you should definitely use effectively what has been given to you. Your gift(s) is not designed to lie dormant or useless.

3. *The Master left--- but trusted his servants to care for and to multiply the resources given.*
   Did you notice the Master did not outline a plan for multiplicity? Yet, the master had an expectation of multiplicity. Upon his return, the Master expected to receive more back than what he actually gave the servants. He gave them something to "work" with. The servants were expected

to be useful, to make good and to multiply the gifts (talents) given to them.

4. ***The reward was the same for each servant as long as the servant produced according to their abilities (capacity).*** They were rewarded according to their stewardship.
It did not matter, rather each servant was given 1, 2 or 5 talents! Eachone who did something with the talent/gift(s) given, actually doubled what was given to them. Consequently, they were rewarded, celebrated and given more. But the useless steward did nothing with what he was given, therefore he received nothing and even what he had buried was taken away!

If the parable is practically applied to life today, we see where human God-ness ----***man's powerful and creative abilities,*** comes into play. Humans really are god's in the earth! Here is where working YOUR part of the plan is required. Gifts have been given to you by the Highest power in the universe–Creator God, but your job is to "work" what He has given you to maximize your purpose and potential in the earth!

In the beginning, man was created. Then Adam was placed in the Garden of Eden---- a place created for Adam's comfort and dominion. It was a place rich with streams and unlimited possibilities. It was the Creator's gift to his creation. It was a world given Adam over which He was to have dominion and stewardship. Then, he gave Adam a responsibility to do something with the gifts He had been entrusted. The expectation was that Adam would use his creative wiring (his gift) –the power within him to manifest the Masters' expectation. His gifts were gifts of creativity and administration whereby he would prove capable of exercising dominion. These gifts would allow Adam to operate in his purpose as a god on the Earth. As each animal was brought to Adam, the Creator said *"whatever you name it, Adam, that's what it will be."* Adam had to dig deep within the wells of his creative nature to come up with a name for everything he saw that was entrusted under his dominion. Can you imagine how much work that was? Can you imagine how much creative energy that required? The Supreme Powers of the universe created each animal but Adam was given dominion (stewardship) over them. He therefore was expected to work with the gifts he was given. When he named them---they would "BE".

What have you named? How are you working? You have got to do something with the gift(s) you have received. Many people are not working in their purpose. Many are not using the gifts they have been given. They have just settled for production on a job—which is not always all together bad as long as you are not allowing the gifts you have been given to lie dormant. This is useless-ness. You cannot be idle with the gifts and talents given you. At some point the expectation is that you would tap into the purposes for which you have been created and multiply that which you have been given. You cannot give all of your energy to someone else's purpose--- often, better known as just a job. (J.O.B. stands for Just over broke.) While your job may afford you many pleasures and a six figure income, there is still an expectation of you from the Gift Giver to use the gifts and talents that you have been given and to multiply them.

What mattered then is what still matters now! MULTIPLICATION of the talents was and is what is expected! **The Master expects that you would use well what you have been given. Then and only then, will you get more. The principle is clear, if you do not use what you have been given, even that which was given will be taken away.**

As I ponder this parable it answers so many questions that I used to have and even responds to my silent musings. "Why does it seem the rich only get richer?" "Why do we have to work so hard for other people?" "Why is the struggle so real? Myra's list of questions over the years could go on and on. But, I now know that I HAVE TO WORK EVERY TALENT…EVERY GIFT AND EVERY STREAM given me! I must exercise good stewardship and multiply what I have been given. Then, and only then will I make my way prosperous and have great success! The world is awaiting us. Let's resist being lazy and useless in this season. The price to be paid for being lazy is far too great. I'm ready for multiplication! How about you?

Scripture Meditations: Matthew 25, Joshua 1:18, John 15

DAY 34: LESSON ON INVESTMENT

Let's look again at the parable from St. Matthew 25:14-30(Message Bible).

The Giver of gifts ---our Creator, has an expectation of multiplicity of the gifts over which we have been given stewardship. When we meet the expectation, there is great reward. When we don't there is great loss. The loss is even greater than what we've initially been given.

The Holy Spirit has made it quite clear to me that as a steward, it is my responsibility to create means of **generational, duplicable, sustainable wealth** for not just me, but for my children's children. I exist for the sole purpose of being a blessing to the lives of men. It would be a waste of Heaven's resources for me to be a blessing while I am alive only. It would be negligent of me. I would not be a wise faithful steward if I died broke. I would not be a wise and faithful steward if I did not die empty without leaving my mark, –my fingerprint in the earth. I would not be a wise and faithful steward if I did not leave an inheritance to my children and if I did not teach them how to follow my example to duplicate themselves in the earth! I must teach my children how to use their gifts and talents to create streams of income and this same heritage must be passed on by them to their children and their children's children. The earth will know that Myra Lynette Davis-Bellinger has been placed as a gift to this world by God, the Creator of the universe. When I die, I will have finished my course! This is a picture of generation, duplicable sustainable wealth! Isn't that an awesome thought and feeling? I can see it. I breathe it. I expect it! I live it!

I shared my intentions and purpose of generational, duplicable and sustainable wealth with someone whose mind had never even thought of such. They were like all too many people who live like hamsters on the wheel of life. They were just existing and barely breathing to live. My thoughts, both perplexed and frustrated them. It was overwhelming because there was in their minds, no way for this to happen to just ordinary people. They agreed that it was an easy feat for those who were fortunate enough to be born with a proverbial silver spoon in their mouths. Sadly, this individual was just a victim of existence! Being able to create means of **generational, duplicatable, sustainable wealth** comes from wise servants who understand their purpose, the power of streams and the power of investments! This is why BREATHING PROPERLY is so important.

There is a place where you can get in life that allows you to live your best life. In this place, your direction is clear. Your capacity is often expanded. You are at peace. You walk in the light. You do the work. Everything is perfect. This place is called alignment. It is when you become in total alignment with the Power of the Universe–the God who created you, ON and WITH purpose. It is not about being busy and doing a lot of stuff. When you live in this place and space things are much easier.. Production is inevitable. Strategies are given. Concepts and timing are understood. Needs seem to be supernaturally met. Increase and multiplication is your portion. And the purposes for which you were created is most definitely fulfilled. This is a place of unexplainable joy. Whenever you are out of alignment with the Power of the Universe---the total opposite occurs and you walk, live, work and exist in total darkness. (See the parable). You stay on the hamsters wheel in life. You seldom experience Heaven on Earth---the fun, beauty, the fulfillment, the pleasure and joy for which your life has been designed.

Life is about investment. Life is about taking risks. It's about investing your gifts--- your time, talents, and resources the right way and in the right places in this world. Life is not to be burdensome. A good indication that you are out of alignment is when the thought of attaining your best life frustrates, saddens and overwhelms you. When you BREATHE PROPERLY and walk in sync with the will of God, you get your marching orders. You get the "WHAT." The "what" is clear direction and clear instruction. I call that receiving "downloads". You will not always get the WHY and the HOW, but that's not your part. You will not always get full instructions. But when you get ANY instructions downloaded to your spirit, be sure to do that instantly. As you obey the little, more will come. What happens is that, intuitively, you just seem to know or hear or get a great idea! **Your job is to release the "what".** *You release the "what" by saying--repeating, believing, doing and expecting what your spirit downloaded to you during your times of BREATHING. The universe will respond to this energy (this faith) that you are releasing by creating the* **"How." It is not your job to figure out HOW the WHAT is going to be done.** That is the job of the Master of the Universe! Just keep breathing, working, obeying, and expecting!

Here are some practical steps to make sure you are investing properly!

1. For best results, refuse to live so cautiously you are afraid to take risks! Life is a journey of faith. When you get the "downloads"—leap! Don't live in fear. It will paralyze you and cause you to be stuck. If you're stuck you're doing nothing or using your energy the wrong way.

2. Don't be like the last servant in the parable. Make sure your heart is right and you are obedient. Do a motive check so your perspective is right. Then you will have a clear vision and precision of steps. You don't have time to waste time and to walk in darkness. Don't spend your life crying and worrying.

3. Know and appreciate the value of your gifts. Do not allow others to devalue you or your gifting's. Expect favor.

4. Know and have an appreciation for your current position in life. Do not despise the vantage point from which you see. Appreciate every situation, every set-back and each triumph. Learn quickly from each experience. Keep investing!

5. As you make investments, know your audience. The grace on your life is not for everyone. There is a grace on your life for those to whom you are assigned. Know who you are called to and then you will always be an "effective working."

Your success hinges on these tips, concepts, alignment and more.. You too, can have great investments that are generational, duplicatable and sustainable.

Today, I decree over you...

The wait is OVER! You are not waiting on success! You are making yourself successful!

The Spirit of entrepreneurship, multiplication and wisdom for streams, with acceleration is upon you! Carpe diem!

Scripture Meditation: Matthew 25:14-30, Joshua 1:8, Hebrews 11:1

BONUS FEATURE

FROM THE HEART OF YOUR FATHER

I hesitated about putting this particular meditation in this book because this book is not just for women. It is for all people. However, the more I thought about it, the more I was inspired to place it in this book. Today's meditation is a love letter from the heart of God, especially written for the woman. But even if you are not a woman, you know a woman. You have a mother, sister, daughter or friend; reading this letter from the Lord's heart to them will bless you. Take your time reading this devotion. Sit down in a relaxed place, get a cup of coffee or tea and imagine having a quiet moment with God as he speaks His heart to you. Enjoy!

From the Lover of Your Soul, the Lord Your Creator

"The Woman: My created but specially shaped and formed vessel. The Woman: RIB, taken out of man but existing to make him complete, for He finds MY favor when he finds you. You were an answer to his NEED, his void. My woman, I am jealous for you. I have taken such special time, extra time in forming you and making you beautiful, special and unique. I had MY time with you in the beginning—just you and Me first—before ever presenting you to him. There, while he was asleep and it was just you and I, I wired you with ME first. You received my DNA. There, in our space, I validated you and assured you of your calling and purpose. It was our special time and then I presented you to him.

Have you ever noticed that within the animal kingdom the male gender stands out differently? He exists in his glory, color, beauty and splendor. It is not the same with you. I have made you, My woman, radiant with glory, full of color, beauty and with the zest and the capacity for all of the fullness of life. I named "wisdom" after you. In our time together, I gave you the capacity for immeasurable inner strength. I placed in your DNA power and multi-tasking, stereo abilities. Yet, I called you "weak." For your strength is made perfect only in yielding and submitting to the Source of it. That source is Me.

You were created to have a special relationship with me. I am your first husband. You are able to "feel" as I feel. You are able to love, worship and nurture with ease. You have strength for childbearing and birthing visions and visionaries. Oh my woman, how I long for you to know who you are, what you can do and the greatness of your capacity in ME. I have a passion and purpose for you. You must remember that I am the source of all your strength and the Author and Finisher of your faith. Do not try to do anything in your life separate from me. Do not leave me as your last resort, but rather, as your first consideration in EVERYTHING. I exist to make life easy for you. Come to me. Ask me. Yield to me and let me live in you and love through you. I love you and all that I created to be. This is from my heart to yours!"

Now after hearing God's heart, surely you know, you have what it takes to make it and succeed in this life.

Scripture Meditations: Proverbs 8:17, Jeremiah 29:11, Romans 5:2-5, Isaiah 54:1-17, Hosea 2:14-17 & 19-20

ABOUT THE AUTHOR

Myra is an author, certified life coach and transformational speaker who has traveled over 30 years assisting businesses and non-profit organizations with organizational structures, training, and development. She inspires individuals to LIVE their BEST life! She is a wife, mother, entrepreneur, and conference host who understands the power of positivity and unity. Myra knows firsthand how powerful lives can be when people take the time to de-clutter and un-busy themselves long enough to take moments to "just breathe!!!" She has an uncanny ability to help people discover how to maximize their potential in the earth. Myra bridges gaps, brings people together to laugh, to motivate and to inspire them to be their BEST unique self.

However, Myra's ultimate joy and humblest ministry lie within her role as a wife and mother. She finds great pride in being married to Gary Bellinger, and together they create a loving home in Mooresville, NC. Their children, David, Maya, Jasmine, Sylver, and Cameron, are a constant source of inspiration and blessings.

To connect with Myra or get booking information email:
Breathewithmyra@gmail.com

Made in the USA
Columbia, SC
09 June 2025